Oral Mentor Texts

A Powerful Tool for
Teaching Reading,
Writing, Speaking,
and Listening

Connie Dierking
Sherra Jones

Foreword by Lester L. Laminack

HEINEMANN
Portsmouth, NH

Heinemann
361 Hanover Street
Portsmouth, NH 03801–3912
www.heinemann.com

Offices and agents throughout the world

© 2014 by Connie Dierking and Sherra Jones

The authors and publisher wish to thank those who have generously given permission to reprint borrowed material:

Excerpts from Common Core State Standards © Copyright 2010. National Governors Association Center for Best Practices and Council of Chief State School Officers. All rights reserved.

Poem "Spaghetti, Spaghetti" from *Rainy, Rainy Saturday* by Jack Prelutsky. Text copyright © 1980 by Jack Prelutsky. Reprinted by permission of HarperCollins Publishers.

Cataloging-in-Publication Data is on file at the Library of Congress.
ISBN: 978-0-325-05358-5

Editor: Zoë Ryder White
Production: Victoria Merecki
Cover and interior designs: Suzanne Heiser
Front cover photos: Zero Creatives/Cultura Collection/Getty Images (*top photo*);
   Debi Fiegle (*bottom photos*)
Typesetter: Publishers' Design & Production Services, Inc.
Manufacturing: Steve Bernier

Printed in the United States of America on acid-free paper
18   17   16   15   14   EBM   1   2   3   4   5

To Madeline:

Let the stories begin!

C. C. D.

———————————— « « » » ————————————

To all of the students I have taught over the years:

Thanks for filling my heart with stories.

S. J.

Contents

All of the appendices are also available for download at www.heinemann.com /products/E05358.aspx (click on the Companion Resources tab).

Foreword

I grew up in the rural South. We are a people of stories. We know who we are and who our people are from the stories we are fed in childhood. Stories sustain us like food, nourish us body and soul. I know relatives I have never met from stories told on porches as daylight slipped into bed under the blanket of night. I have insights into the childhood of my mother from stories my aunts told to the rhythm of a porch swing. I know a life before electricity and running water, when children worked the fields and learned to hunt to help keep food in the bellies of their siblings. I know these things from stories told to the cadence of tree frogs and the mournful call of the whippoorwill.

Stories are powerful magic in every culture. They conjure up a past that predates our existence. They reanimate experiences that lie dormant in our psyche, events we have moved beyond. They connect us one to another, a quilt of humanity. Stories keep relationships and emotions and experience alive and thriving. Stories help us understand ourselves and others. Stories tether us to place, ground us with a sense of belonging. Stories serve as touchstones when we have difficult decisions to make. They are mentors from our past, our culture, and our shared experience with trusted others. We return to our stories over and over throughout our lives like a child with a security blanket.

Oral Mentor Texts: A Powerful Tool for Teaching Reading, Writing, Speaking, and Listening harnesses the age-old power of storytelling within whole-class "oral mentor texts"—teaching texts that students practice and internalize, a host of mentors in common, always on hand to support their reading and writing throughout the year. Connie and Sherra give us a clear, logical, elegantly simple process for creating oral mentor texts in the classroom to use alongside printed mentor texts to guide and support literacy instruction. They start by selecting a moment the entire class has shared. Next they write it down, carefully embedding craft details and teachable content they will form lessons around. Finally they incorporate it into their literacy teaching as an oral mentor text. As students internalize and retell the story, Connie and Sherra use it to teach craft techniques and skills—leads, endings, dialogue, vocabulary, summarization, inferring, as well as listening and oral-language skills, to mention just a few.

Oral mentor texts are personal, accessible, and intimately understood. They are stories of a shared experience tucked into the pockets of each child's heart and soul. They become the security blanket, the familiar and trusted resource that informs and influences each child's knowledge of story grammar, structure, purpose, word choice, sentence variation, tone, and voice. They are with each student every day, all day. They influence how children approach printed mentor texts and how they construct their own writing.

Oral mentor texts offer something fresh and accessible in this era of increasing demands as we struggle to ensure that our students can access learning in ways that honor their humanity. While creating a level playing field may be beyond our reach, we can and we must create some common ground for all students. Connie and Sherra build on traditions of sound practice and common sense to develop patches of common ground from which our students can move forward in their learning journey.

Lester Laminack
Asheville, NC / Beaufort, SC

Acknowledgments

We have many stories to tell—after all, we are teachers, mothers, wives, sisters, friends. Every day, our lives are filled with small moments, unexpected happenings, and unique experiences that we weave into stories to be savored and remembered. We know that storytelling is best when the storyteller engages with an audience. We were very lucky that our editor, Zoë Ryder White, was a member of the audience we spoke to one spring day at the International Reading Association Conference. We were over-the-moon excited about the life-changing method of instruction we had embraced. After our talk, we met Zoë and knew we had found a soul mate. We thank her for understanding that stories are the foundation for not only living well but for reading, writing, speaking, and listening well. So we begin with a heartfelt thank you to you, Zoë.

Thank you to Natalie Louis for sharing her fireman story and introducing us to the power of a shared story.

Thank you to the coaches and teachers of Pinellas County Schools for your interest in learning ways of incorporating oral storytelling into your day and for sharing your own stories of success.

Thank you to our principal, Pam Metz-Easley, for never tempering our enthusiasm.

Thank you to our friends and colleagues at Curtis Fundamental Elementary who listened to each one of our class stories and delighted in the simplicity of small children sharing an event.

Thank you to both Maria DeWeiss and Cristi Bakewell for accepting oral storytelling with open arms and trusting us to give it a go.

Thank you to Debi Fiegle for her beautiful photographs of storytellers in action.

Thank you to our own personal mentors, those friends and fellow educators who have been with us always, no matter where we hung our work hat.

Thank you to our wonderful students who brought the stories to life, both in the air and on paper. And thank you to their parents for listening with bright eyes.

Thank you to our families for never complaining about the nights and weekends we were completely unavailable. You have our unending gratitude.

We feel fortunate that we were able to initiate, sustain, and finally complete this labor of love. Find *your* story, tell it loud and tell it clear. The benefits are priceless.

Introduction

Not Just Stories, but Oral Mentor Texts

I t seems that summer is the only time we can finish conversations begun during the school year. Even after teaching together for more than twenty years, we look forward to summer days—not only for the time to breathe and recharge, but also for the clarity of thought a little distance from the school year can bring. Although we have taught in the same school, often in classrooms right next to each other, carving out the time for deep reflection can be tricky. Spending summers batting ideas back and forth, scouring professional journals, and talking, talking, and even more talking usually leads to fresh ideas. In fact, one of these summers led us to an epiphany: Oral storytelling could support our literacy curriculum.

That summer, Connie attended her first summer institute at the Teacher's College Reading and Writing Project. She remembers listening intently to staff developer Natalie Louis describing how her first graders had composed a letter to the firemen housed near her school, thanking them for their service in the aftermath of the 9/11 tragedy. For Natalie's class, it was the delivery of the letter—the class' physical journey to the fire station—that became the heart of the experience for the class. Natalie marveled at how her students asked her to retell the story of the letter delivery over and over again. She discovered that the power of this shared experience influenced other areas of literacy in the classroom. This story became a shared oral text. Students learned how to retell the story themselves, and Natalie was able to teach into their retellings in order to support comprehension development in reading and writing.

We had both used storytelling in our classrooms, but this was different. Using a retold shared experience as a classroom mentor text sounded like the answer to some big questions we had been asking ourselves and each other for a very long time:

» What could we do to provide a greater scaffold for our ELL students and students in earlier stages of language development?

» How could we offer a mentor text that students would know so intimately that they would be able to call it up in their minds when needed?

» How could we make the stories students create in their school life support the stories they will encounter in their forever life?

» How could we harness the power of oral language to enrich our students' comprehension?

Our first oral stories were born on the first day of school that year. A huge storm rolled in off the Gulf of Mexico. The dark clouds hovered overhead as Sherra's first-grade students rushed to the classroom from their Art special. Connie's third-grade students noticed the storm brewing from the classroom. This was the opportunity we were looking for: a shared experience that would be exciting to retell. Each of us crafted a story about this shared experience and began teaching the stories to our students the next day.

Sherra's class story went like this:

> Yesterday was the first day of school. At the end of the day, we had art with Mr. Prankard. Just before 2:00, Mrs. Jones picked us up. "Hurry," she warned, "it's about to rain." As we walked to the car line, we noticed the gray clouds in the sky. The thunder rumbled. We wondered if we would make it to our cars before the storm.

Here is Connie's class story:

> The sky grew dark, blocking out the sun that had shone all day. The first day of school had been uneventful, until now. Val peeked out the window as she gathered her new lunchbox and backpack, ready to head home. "Whoa, look at the sky!" she announced. Everyone turned toward the windows. Black clouds raced by and there was lightning on the horizon. Karei mumbled, "It looks really bad out there." Jabari said, "I sure hope we get to our cars before it starts to rain." Mrs. Dierking answered hopefully, "I'm sure you will if we all hurry." And with that we grabbed our stuff and raced out the door like a flash.

As the year progressed and we began using class stories in a variety of ways, we came to recognize how effective the class story was as an oral mentor text, so we began to implement oral language practice through storytelling as part of our literacy curriculum. We watched our students—all of them—speak with expression and confidence as they retold the story. Several students wrote the story during writer's workshop, all on their own. During reader's workshop, students made connections between storylines in the books they read and their class story. The class story was proving to be the mortar for building the bridge between the stories students tell and the stories they read and write. We were sold; oral storytelling had great potential for not only early language learners and ELL learners, but for *all* learners.

As we implemented oral storytelling in support of our students' literacy growth, colleagues became curious as well, and we realized that all classrooms could benefit from this work. We understood that not only must we have a plan for choosing which stories to turn into oral stories, but we had to know how to incorporate district goals and guidelines. What's more, we had to make sure that we were creating a system that would be replicable, not just tied to our particular classrooms and students. We didn't want oral storytelling to be just another thing for teachers to implement; rather, we wanted to ensure that we were practicing oral language authentically in a way that would enhance instruction in all areas of literacy. So, in our second year of implementation, we began to take notes on our process so that we could answer questions like:

» How do I choose an event to turn into an oral story?

» Why do I write the story myself?

» What do I include in an oral story?

» How do I teach my students the stories?

» How do I help students practice the stories?

» Which parts of my day will be the most conducive for teaching the oral story?

» How do I make explicit connections between student class stories and the stories of others?

» Which text types can be used in oral stories? Could I build an explanatory or opinion story as well as a narrative?

» Can I align class stories with literacy standards?

As we became more explicit and deliberate in finding, building, and using the oral class stories, the benefits for students became even more apparent. Students were pointing out everyday occurrences as topics for class stories. Walking to lunch became an exercise in finding a story along the way. Paul accused Mem Fox, a favorite picture book author of ours, of copying our class story's sound lead. Posting story language on the wall as a resource for reading and writing was becoming an everyday occurrence. The class story was seeping into our literacy block and becoming a strong support for our literacy teaching.

Since that second year we have fine-tuned the process and have developed the method you will read about in this book. In a nutshell, the steps of the oral storytelling process are these:

1. **Identify a shared experience.**
2. **Build the story.** Compose the experience into an oral story, keeping in mind your students' needs as well as literacy goals and guidelines identified by your school or district. *(This is done by the teacher, in preparation for literacy instruction with students. In this way, you decide what skills are to be taught and which craft moves the mentor story will help your students practice.)*
3. **Practice the story.** Using predictable structures of gestures and symbols, students learn the story and are able to recite it from memory.
4. **Perform the story.** Presenting the story to an audience is the publication.
5. **Use the story** as a scaffold for comprehension during reading and writing.

What Do We Mean by Oral Mentor Texts?

Of course, there are myriad wonderful ways to use oral storytelling in the classroom. We want to make clear the distinctions between the method we propose—using a teacher-crafted story of a shared class experience as a mentor text—and the many other kinds of storytelling. Teachers often think of storytelling as simply retelling a story that was either read aloud or read independently. This kind of storytelling might include dramatization of the story. Fountas and Pinnell (2006) encourage this type of storytelling as an assessment of comprehension. Story retelling helps teachers determine whether students can grasp the main idea of a story and describe the main events. Gretchen Owocki (2003) thinks of retelling as a way to help children rethink their way through a text, thereby enhancing their understanding.

In other cases, storytelling can mean asking students to retell a family story, the kind of story that can be passed down from generation to generation. With our method of storytelling, a teacher-written shared classroom experience resembles a family story so that it speaks to a student's own experience. The difference, however, besides being the story of a shared class experience, is that we build the story so that it is repeated the same way across retellings. (In my house, for example, the telling of my dad's catch-of-the-day varies, from the prize being as small as a pinfish to one as large as a shark—it just depends on who is telling the story!)

Another brilliant form of storytelling, developed by Vivian Gussin Paley (1990), is based on students dictating their own invented stories to the teacher, which are then dramatized by the students and their classmates. Paley views storytelling as an extension of play, and an opportunity for each child's story to be celebrated by the classroom community.

Finally, there is the language experience approach to storytelling. The Language Experience Approach (LEA) stems from the work of Lilliam Lamoreaux and Doris Lee (1963) and Sylvia Ashton-Warner's work with Maori children in New Zealand (1963). This approach requires students to choose an experience to be dictated to the teacher. The words are chosen by the students and recorded on a sheet of paper for all to see. The teacher doesn't compose the text to reinforce or practice previous skills or strategies, or to align with grade-level standards. The story is composed for students to read. The central principle of LEA is to use the students' own vocabulary, language patterns, and experiences to create their own reading texts. The text unfolds in front of them as they dictate what they want the teacher to record. Although the oral component is important to building the story, the main focus of this kind of storytelling is to create a written text.

Our method serves a different purpose though. While students do perform the class oral story, the story is teacher-composed, based on a shared class experience, and stocked with specific skills and craft moves that will support students in their current reading and writing work. Our stories are literally designed to be oral mentor texts. Built deliberately by the teacher, the stories teach, reinforce, and practice identified skills and strategies. Once practiced and performed, students internalize the story so that it lives in their memories as a mentor text for both reading and writing. The story belongs to the students, remaining with them forever and lighting the way whenever they get stuck.

But How Can I Fit It In?

Many teachers have asked us, "How do I fit this in?" We always respond with, "Can you find ten minutes a day?" All you need is ten minutes. Just block off ten minutes right before lunch or right before students go home in the afternoon. Or practice the story during classroom transitions—students can tell the story as they line up for the lunchroom or the gym.

The class story doesn't have to take a lot of time. You determine the structures that work for you based on how much time you have. Building the class story will take some thought, but the standards and curriculum requirements you incorporate are part of your teaching and planning anyway. And once the story is celebrated and sent out into the world, you can use it as a mentor text for whole-class or small-group reading and writing instruction and in individual conferences. Once stories are in kids' memories, they have them to enjoy, share, and use forever.

The oral class story is also cost effective: It's free! It's an authentic way to incorporate speaking and listening standards into reading and writing instruction. The class story is engaging, builds confidence, and will be remembered for years to come. All of this in exchange for ten minutes a day! When a colleague asked Sherra how she found the time to incorporate the class story into her literacy block, Sherra responded, "How could I not?"

How to Use This Book

Chapter 1 explains why we so deeply value oral storytelling as a form of composition and as a method of literacy instruction. We'll provide a summary of how use of class stories—oral mentor texts—generally unfolds across the year, moving from finding and building a class story to learning and practicing the story. We will show you how a story can grow and change along with the needs of your students and your sequence of instruction. Chapter 2 describes the process of choosing and "building" the class story. In Chapter 3 we continue with structures for introducing and practicing the story as a class. After the story is found, built, and practiced it becomes a tool for teaching. In Chapters 4 and 5, we give an overview of how skills embedded in the class story transfer into students' writing and reading work. We also include four categories of minilessons that we use during our transfer instruction. A barebones minilesson from each category along with a list of potential teaching points for use as support for reading or writing conferences will help get you started. Chapter 6 focuses on how to support your students as they choose and compose their own oral stories, in partnerships and individually. After all, this is the prize: watching our students spread their wings and fly, carrying their *very own* stories with them and calling upon these stories as their *very own* resource wherever they may be! Many chapters will contain a section discussing the specific needs of ELL students. We will also link this storytelling work to the Common Core State Standards.

Child psychologist Jerome Bruner wrote, "We are storytelling creatures, and as children we acquire language to tell those stories that we have inside us" (1985). Oral language is the foundation for comprehension. Using class stories as oral mentor texts will allow comprehension to begin where it is most natural and innate—the story itself.

The Gasp Heard 'Round the Media Center: The Thirty Million Word Gap

A few years ago our principal shared the results of a vocabulary study during our back-to-school staff meeting. After conducting research in the homes of preschool children in Kansas City, Betty Hart and Todd Risley (1995) confirmed that while children from different backgrounds typically develop language skills around the same age, the subsequent rate of vocabulary growth is strongly influenced by how much parents talk to their children. They also found that children in professional families, whose parents talk to them more, increase their vocabulary at a quicker rate than their peers in working-class and welfare-recipient families. They dubbed this disparity "the thirty million word gap." The teachers gathered in our media center gasped: Thirty million words are an inconceivably high number. The two of us once again came face to face with the question we had been asking each other for years: What can we do to help children bridge this cavernous gap?

Even though we can't influence the experiences students have before they enter our classrooms, we can be more deliberate about the language experiences they have while in it. As kindergarten teachers, we had been discouraged year after year by the number of children who entered our classrooms in August and left them in June still struggling to communicate. Although we had no curriculum and no time in the day to deliberately teach either receptive or expressive language skills, our literacy leaders assured us that by reading aloud and talking with our students, we were teaching

Cambourne's Conditions for Learning

IMMERSION

Students need to be immersed in a language-rich environment. The classroom should contain language-rich posters, charts, student work, displays, classroom libraries, and so forth, and students should hear lots of talk and stories read aloud.

DEMONSTRATION

Students need demonstrations throughout the day of complex receptive and expressive language.

ENGAGEMENT

Students must actively engage with language while learning, and learning must be active, not a spectator sport. Opportunities to use language in authentic ways must be provided.

EXPECTATION

Students learn in an environment in which the teacher communicates high expectations, believing that the student can and will use language in many ways and situations.

USE

Students need to use their knowledge in their everyday lives. They are expected to apply this new knowledge today and every day.

APPROXIMATION

Students should feel free to take risks with their learning. They must experience success in a safe, supportive environment. They should feel that their efforts will not be judged as imperfect.

RESPONSE

Students need to receive feedback on their language use from significant others at school and at home.

(Adapted from Brian Cambourne's *The Whole Story: Natural Learning and the Acquisition of Literacy in the Classroom.*)

Figure 1.1 Brian Cambourne's Conditions for Learning

these skills implicitly. While this is true up to a point, we knew this approach was not helping all students succeed. We knew we needed to teach these skills explicitly as well as implicitly. After considering the conditions of learning identified by Brian Cambourne in his work with language acquisition (see Figure 1.1), we decided to provide our students with language support through the telling of shared experiences.

Teaching Oral Language Skills Explicitly

Sharing news or retelling a favorite book every day immerses students in language. Even before beginning our work with classroom stories, we used appropriate language, and we encouraged our students to approximate and use appropriate language while speaking, listening, reading, and writing. Students always received feedback from us and from their classmates.

However, this wasn't enough to help those students who had entered school behind their peers catch up. A case in point: One afternoon Sherra assembled her students on the rug and read aloud *Our Tree Named Steve*, by Alan Zweibel (2005). In this story, two-year-old Sari can't pronounce the word *tree*, so she calls the tree in her yard *Steve*. As Sari grows up, the tree, Steve, plays an important part in her life. In the end Steve has to be cut down but is remembered with fondness forever. The story prompted much talk about family, getting older, special objects, and the like. As the discussion was winding down, Emma raised her hand: "Mrs. Jones, who is Steve?" All the conditions were present for Emma to comprehend the story. What had gone wrong? And what could Sherra do to help her?

The Importance of Retelling

Retelling a text increases both the quantity and quality of comprehension. It requires a number of skills, including inferring, determining importance, visualizing, and summarizing. Retelling not only is an important strategy for deepening comprehension but also enhances language development and communication skills (Benson and Cummins 2000).

Robert Munsch is a favorite author in Sherra's first-grade classroom. Her students love to listen to their classmates retell *Stephanie's Ponytail* (1996). Recently, small groups reenacted the antics of Stephanie and her ponytail. Each group retold the story a little differently. One group emphasized the different ways Stephanie wears her ponytail. Another zeroed in on how her classmates copy her hairstyle. No group retold the story exactly the same way, but all the groups retold the story succinctly, in the proper order. Participating in the retelling helped the students in each group to do the following:

» Develop storytelling language
» Organize thought into a sequential story
» Pay attention to detail
» Recite sentences of different length
» Lay an important foundation for understanding story elements
» Retrieve and pronounce words

Retelling gives readers an opportunity to process what they have read by organizing the information and explaining it to others.

This can be difficult for beginning readers, who are often confused by the sequence of events. The Max and Ruby series, by Rosemary Wells, were favorites in one of Connie's kindergarten classes. She introduced *Max's Birthday* (2004) in an engaging, interactive read-aloud. In the story Max receives a wind-up toy lobster for his birthday from his sister Ruby. Max is afraid of the lobster because it chases him around the room. Finally Max falls and the lobster stops right on top of his tummy. Discovering that he likes the toy lobster after all, Max says, "Again!"

Ryan struggled with his retelling: "It was his birthday. He was chasing the lobster. He got a lobster. He had a birthday. He liked the lobster. He got a lobster. It was his birthday." He saw the book as separate events, not as a whole, with no links between the birthday, the lobster, and Max. There was no story grammar, no ability to determine what was important. Ryan needed explicit instruction in how to tell a story and then additional time to practice.

The value of teaching students to retell stories multiple times is clear. For example, kindergartners Melissa and John are retelling *The Three Billy Goats Gruff* in the puppet center. After retelling the story once, Melissa wants to retell it again. They begin arguing about how many billy goats will go over the bridge. Melissa is certain that three goats will go over; John is convinced that because they've told the story once, all the goats are already gone. As Melissa holds up the first billy goat puppet and starts the story, John says, "That's not him. The troll went over the bridge and he is gone. We already told that story!" For John, the story happens once and that's it. The goats are gone, no need for retelling. John has not yet internalized the idea that an event in a story can be told over and over as if happening for the first time. We can teach him that rewinding a story and reliving it again is at the heart of living as a literate being.

Going About It

We began by teaching our students how to retell a familiar story. We read and reread aloud picture books with a strong storyline and then had students retell these stories to a partner using picture support. Many of them sounded as if they were reading the words. Elizabeth Sulzby (1991) identified eleven stages that students go through on the way to conventional reading, and we saw our students progressing along this continuum. (See Figure 1.2 for a summarized description.)

Their retellings helped us assess their comprehension of familiar stories. We began to wonder what would happen if their own stories sounded like they came from a book. What if their *own* stories became mentor texts?

Elizabeth Sulzby's Stages of Emergent Storybook Reading

STAGES 1 & 2
Retelling includes labels and comments, following the action.

STAGES 3 & 4
Student tells a story with a sense of beginning, middle, and end using story language and syntax.

STAGES 5–7
Retelling is still picture-based; student begins to sound like a reader but is not yet watching the print (still relying on memory).

STAGES 8–10
Child begins to say "I can't read this" because of developing awareness of print; some aspects of conventional reading begin to combine with the previous picture-based retellings.

STAGE 11
Student demonstrates conventional reading behavior with a familiar book.

(From Wiley Online Library)

Figure 1.2 Elizabeth Sulzby's Stages of Emergent Storybook Reading

Telling a story is the foundation for writing a story, and some children need to have that foundation shored up. Recall the puzzled look that sometimes comes across a student's face after you ask, "How's it going?"

You: "How's it going?"

Student: "I wrote right here that I love my dog."

You: "Wow, I see that." *[Pointing to the accompanying drawing]* "Is this your dog?"

Student: "That's my dog."

You: "So what's going on here with your dog? Tell me the story."

Student: *[Stares at the teacher]*

Our students come to school bursting to tell the stories of their lives. Andrew rushes in on Monday morning: "Mrs. Dierking, I lost a tooth yesterday. It came out when I was eating breakfast and I almost swallowed it." Xavier rushes in on Tuesday morning: "Mrs. Jones, my cat ran away and I made a poster to put up on the street light by my house!" On Wednesday morning Blake confides, "Mrs. Dierking, my sister put a pea up her nose and she had to go to the emergency room!" Thursday: "Mrs. Jones, we saw a fire truck on our way to school!" Children can't wait to tell us these important moments in their daily lives, and this is a wonderful thing. But often the stories either stop after the first couple of sentences or they go on and on and on.

This is fine when students are sharing informally. But so many students need support in retelling their stories sequentially, succinctly, and with detail. Without being able to tell or retell a story out loud—"in the air"—it is very difficult to compose a story on paper. Being able to tell a story in sequential order in the excitement and exhilaration of the moment is a powerful skill. Telling a story coherently helps students write a coherent story.

As we contemplated using oral stories as the starting point for our literacy instruction, we quickly realized we couldn't listen to a whole classroom of individual stories during the first few weeks of school. So, we borrowed a technique from Lamoreaux, Lee, and Ashton-Warner (1963) in which students jointly compose a story while the teacher acts as scribe. We use a similar type of shared experience but formulate the story orally.

Through this shared event we teach and reinforce vocabulary, story grammar, and structure. Students are also able to practice speaking and listening. Orally retelling a common school experience is the scaffold students need to be able to retell someone else's story. They also deepen their comprehension by looking at a story from the inside out. Children want to know what makes something tick. The act of simply drawing a cat or a tree will lead to the question, "How did you do that?" The inquiring mind of a child wants to know the inside work of reading. Orally retelling a common school experience allows students to peek inside a story and bear witness to where stories come from. This scaffold allows them to tell and retell their own stories and eventually empowers them to write these stories down with coherence.

In *A Quick Guide to Making Your Teaching Stick, K–5* (2008), Shanna Schwartz stresses the importance of using stories as powerful connectors between our children and the strategies we want to teach them. Telling stories again and again throughout the day draws students in. They lean toward us, watching our faces, excited to connect in this very personal way. Schwartz writes, "In a magical minilesson, the teaching doesn't seem as if it is for any ol' class; it feels custom fit for this class." The story provides the connection.

Another powerful connector is putting students themselves into a story. Chronicling a child's positive actions paves the way for others to try the same thing. Using the name of a student in a class story turns him or her into a famous storybook character. Using a story about *this* class builds community, setting the stage for the students' own storytelling and story writing.

Initially presenting a shared experience to students as an oral story enhances their understanding of "how a story goes." Having all children experience the story's creation firsthand is the glue that makes the important components of retelling stick. Examples of oral stories are presented in Figure 1.3.

As we continued retelling shared experiences as if they were stories in a book, we noticed patterns in students' responses. Whatever we did deliberately when we retold a shared class experience, many students copied in their own retellings. After Sherra began an oral story with "One hot sunny day at the park," her students began their retellings with that setting. When Connie highlighted transition words, students began using them as well. These oral mentor texts are the scaffold the students need to embrace other retelling strategies as well, such as making predictions, asking and answering questions, and providing a sense of story and prosody.

A Typical Initial Story for First Grade

Remember the story Sherra shared in the introduction?

> Yesterday was the first day of school. At the end of the day, we had art with Mr. Prankard. Just before 2:00, Mrs. Jones picked us up. "Hurry!" she warned. "It is about to rain." As we walked to the car line we noticed gray clouds in the sky. The thunder rumbled. We wondered if we would make it to our cars before it started to rain.

She retold an event the students had experienced together as a story they could then retell to someone else. When presenting this story, she had a general idea of what she might want students to practice in an oral story. She considered its length and the way the sentences were structured and included dialogue and a few strong verbs.

A Typical Initial Story for Third Grade

As we began to compose more and more oral stories, we were more strategic in planning the retellings.

> It is hard to believe we are in third grade. Some friends we already know, but some friends are new. We were just settling in to get to know each other when the loudest noise we had ever heard came across the intercom. It sounded like a wounded duck. "What is going on?" inquired Mrs. Dierking. Everyone was holding their hands over their ears. The sound, *akkk-akkk-akkk*, wouldn't stop. Mrs. Dierking flung open the door and asked Mrs. Stewart if she knew what was happening. Mrs. Stewart's students were acting just like we were! Their hands were over their ears and their mouths were shaped in a big round O. Both teachers huddled in the hallway discussing the matter. Finally, just as we were about to leave our room and possibly the building to get away from that atrocious noise, it stopped. What an interesting way to start third grade. We are going to call it "The Year of the Duck."

In this retelling of a shared event, Connie included varied sentences and a spot in the story to practice showing, not telling. She deliberately included the literacy skills she wanted her students to hear and practice.

Figure 1.3 Samples of Oral Stories

In *Teaching for Deep Comprehension* (2005), Linda Dorn and Carla Soffos note: "Children involved in talk that includes retelling an event using language that includes setting, characters, events, and an ending is an important precursor to comprehension. This is quite simply a story. The potential of storytelling through narrative discourse will assist with growing comprehension skills." We have found that telling a story benefits all children, from emergent readers and beyond, as they expand their ability to use language to make meaning.

Dorn and Soffos identify ten strategic behaviors that link oral language and comprehension:

1. Manipulating forms of speech to express meaning
2. Making good word choices that communicate clear messages
3. Using pronouns to stand for nouns
4. Using punctuation to clarify meaning and regulate fluency
5. Combining simple sentences into more complex ones
6. Organizing related ideas into paragraphs, chapters, texts, and genre
7. Using dialogue to carry and extend meaning
8. Using figurative language to symbolize meaning
9. Building vocabulary through word relationships and patterns
10. Using transitional words and phrases

We need to both teach these behaviors and then show students how they work together to make meaning. When we ask children to tell the story of something that has happened to them, we are teaching strategic behaviors.

These behaviors influence students' acquisition of the forms and functions of language that support comprehension. They must manipulate phonemes to form words, use precise words to convey meaning to their listener, and speak with fluency. Their story must be organized and retold in an order that makes sense, and it may include figurative language and dialogue to make it more interesting. Story, in its broadest sense, is the retelling of a set of related events. Retelling a story encompasses important comprehension strategies, including making connections, visualizing, and summarizing. Background knowledge, vocabulary knowledge, language structures, verbal reasoning, and literacy knowledge provide the foundation for literacy learning. Retelling a story provides practice in all these strategies. Retelling a story that belongs to you provides incredible bang for your buck!

Although telling a story does not require students to read print, it does require them to make meaning and speak with fluency. How many times have we noticed that students who do not read or write fluently do not speak fluently? Retelling a shared event puts speaking fluently first. Give it a try!

Oral Mentor Texts Throughout the Year

Finding and building an oral class story begins on day one. One rule of thumb we follow is that in every class story, everyone must be present in the event being represented. The initial story is a simple event the class has experienced during the first few days of school—getting in line for lunch, walking to the gym, getting a drink from the water fountain. It probably won't be the most exciting thing that happens all year, but it sets the stage. This story is short, sequenced, and told as if it were a story in a book. The goal is to show students that anything that happens to you can be retold, that events should be told in the order they happened, and that there are particular ways stories go when they are being told. First you retell the story to your students. Then the students retell the story again and again until they are very familiar with how it goes. (This goal does not change, from kindergarten through third grade.)

At the same time, students begin to internalize narrative story structure as they read and listen to the stories of well-loved authors. One day Connie began an oral retelling with, "It was the first full day of first grade." Later, first grader Andrea pointed out that the first sentence of *Kitten's First Full Moon* (Henkes 2004) begins, "It was Kitten's first full moon." She squealed with excitement: "Look, Kevin Henkes started his story just like ours!"

A second oral class story is presented about a month into the school year. After finding and building the first oral story, the second one comes together much more quickly. This second story should introduce any skills or strategies students will soon encounter during reading and writing instruction. If your upcoming unit of study emphasizes characters, make sure your oral story mentions character traits. If you will be introducing a particular element of the writer's craft, include it in your story. Keep this second story about the same length as the first but make the sentences more complex. (Chapter 2 lays out the process of explicitly building the story.)

During the next three months, continue to find events to turn into oral class stories to retell, a new one every month. Vary genres to match the text type students are reading and writing. If you are studying nonfiction, insert a little how-to section in your story. By now students should have internalized the process and begun to rely on the oral story as a mentor text for their own reading and writing.

You will also be able to use the class story as a kind of formative assessment of students' writing. In the example in Figure 1.4, Kendall uses the words from a familiar poem to add voice to her piece. The class story used the poem "Spaghetti, Spaghetti" as an attention grabber, so Kendall pumps up her own written story with "Rock-a-Bye Baby." The strategy stuck!

During the last few months of school, students can find and build class stories with a partner. Have the partners identify an event that happened to the two of them, build the story together, practice retelling it, and then retell the story to the rest of the class.

When Sherra's first graders begin finding and retelling shared stories with a partner, they first do things together. If one partner goes to the media center, the other

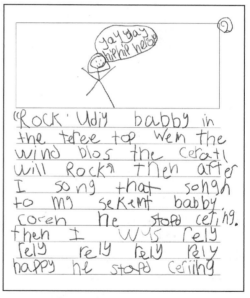

Wah, wah, wah! One starry night my second baby cousin started to cry. Then my Aunt Debby picked him up and carried him around. Then I started singing him a lullaby. "Rock-a-bye baby in the tree top. When the wind blows the cradle will rock." Then after I sang that song to my second baby cousin he stopped crying. Then I was really, really, really, really happy he stopped crying.

Figure 1.4 Kendall's Story

Building Castles
A Partnership Story

TOLD BY: JOSHUA DEWESE AND IAN SIEBERT

One day, we were working as busy as bees trying to build castles out of cardboard. We were in our gifted class. We built a real working drawbridge. Mrs. Allen, our gifted teacher, helped us make a portcullis. A portcullis is a metal gate to keep people out of the castle walls. We worked until Mrs. Allen said, "Let's share!" The first table made a cannon out of plastic balls. The next table was awesome too. They built walls made out of paper and cardboard. Their drawbridge was made out of paper too. But ours was the best of them all! We shared our castle with the four flags, the real working drawbridge, and the portcullis that Mrs. Allen helped us build. It was a fun but exhausting day.

Figure 1.5 Building Castles

partner goes along. Partners sit next to each other at lunch and play the same games at recess. They deliberately search for a happening in common. Once they find their shared event, they build their stories using everything they have learned about retelling a story with clarity and craft. Obviously, Sherra supports the partners during individual conferences, but the content of the stories comes from the students. Topics include playing kickball games during P.E., observing caterpillars on the sidewalk, or creating art projects. Of course, many partnerships choose the same topics (everyone plays kickball and works on art projects). Every partnership creates a story grid. Stories include similar structures. Every partnership performs their story. However, the stories differ in the details: point of view, emphasis, craft elements, and sentence structure. (See Figures 1.5 and 1.6.)

During the last month of school, students should be able to tell their own story following the same process: finding, building, practicing. These stories highlight how

Playing Tag
A Partnership Story

TOLD BY: MICHAELA HAWTHORNE AND MAIJA MILLER

The other day at recess, Michaela and I were playing tag. We were chasing each other around a tree. All of a sudden, Michaela tripped over her shoe laces and fell down. "Ouch, I hurt my knee!" she screamed. I took her to the clinic for a bandage. When we returned to recess, Mrs. Manley said to Michaela, "Now you know why it is important to keep your shoes tied!"

Figure 1.6 Playing Tag

One day my cat came inside our house with a dead lizard in her mouth. She wanted to show off her skills. The lizard was big and brown. I yelled, "Mocha, get that lizard out of your mouth right now." Mocha didn't listen. Then she went back outside and ate the lizard. Me, my mom and dad all said, "Ew, that's gross!"

Figure 1.7 Jonah's Story

much students have learned about the process of storytelling, not just someone else's but theirs (see Figure 1.7).

It has a beginning, a middle, and an end. He has elaborated using size and color words. He also uses dialogue, a craft element that has deliberately been used in every oral class story. Jonah retold this story with excitement and confidence, just as he had practiced when retelling the shared class stories. Jonah has internalized the skills he has been introduced to and practiced.

Figure 1.8 lays out loosely how the oral story changes throughout the year no matter the grade level. Building the story involves layering. Whatever you include in one month should be reinforced in future months. An analogy helps make the point: When making a cake, you have the dry ingredients of flour, sugar, and baking soda. Then you add the wet ingredients, eggs, butter, and vanilla. It takes all of them to make a cake. The chart lists the dry ingredients. The skills and strategies stipulated by your curriculum are the wet ingredients. You can also add chocolate or nuts or fruit—analogous to state and district benchmarks. Chapter 2 discusses how these benchmarks are considered in building the oral story.

You need to stock your stories with the work that you want your students to practice. Month one is about getting started with a story; by month two you will add craft to your story that matches what you are studying in reading or writing. In first grade, you might add a simile and a sound word. In third grade, you might try different transition words that you would like to see your students use in their own narratives. Every month, bump up your story. By the end of the year, no matter the grade, you will probably want to have students, with a partner or individually, find, build, and practice an oral story (see Chapter 2).

How Oral Stories Evolve Across the Year

Oral Story 1	Oral Story 2	Oral Story 3	Oral Story 4
• Simple story line • Shared group experience • Sentence structure that matches age group of class • Dialogue	• A few more sentences • Example of craft • Transition words	• Different type of beginning than previous stories • All narrative elements • New examples of craft	• Structure to match the genre being studied in reading and writing
Oral Story 5	**Oral Story 6**	**Oral Story 7 (partners)**	**Oral Story 8 (individuals)**
• A few more sentences • Varied sentences • Different type of ending than in previous stories • New examples of craft	• Showing, not telling	• Shared experience • All the components of the previous stories	• Personal experience • All the components of the previous stories

Figure 1.8 How Oral Stories Evolve Across the Year

Common Core State Standards Supported

READING STANDARDS FOR LITERATURE

CCRL.K.2—With prompting and support, retell familiar stories, including key details.

CCRL.K.3—With prompting and support, identify characters, settings, and major events in a story.

CCRL.1.2—Retell stories, including key details, and demonstrate understanding of their central message.

CCRL.1.3—Describe characters, settings, and major events in a story, using key details.

CCRL.2.4—Describe how words and phrases (e.g., regular beats, alliteration, rhymes, repeated lines) supply rhythm and meaning in a story, poem, or song.

CCSL.K.4—Describe familiar people, places, things, and events, and, with prompting and support, provide additional detail.

SPEAKING AND LISTENING

CCSL.K.6—Speak audibly and express thoughts, feelings, and ideas clearly.

CCSL.1.4—Describe people, places, things, and events with relevant details, expressing ideas and feelings clearly.

CCSL.2.4—Tell a story or recount an experience with appropriate facts and relevant, descriptive details, speaking audibly in coherent sentences.

Supporting English Language Learners

Oral storytelling is particularly beneficial for English language learners (ELLs) (see Figure 1.9). Being part of the experience on which the story is based, they are "in the story." When listening as the experience is told back to them, they hear the words that represent the experience. Retelling a shared event that happened in real time doesn't present the same constraints as retelling a story derived from print. ELLs can use sensory cues to retell the story. For example, in Sherra's oral class story about leaving art class as a storm moves in, Marco heard the thunder. He knew that the part in the story where the thunder rumbled comes after he left art class. He witnessed the visuals—the dark sky, the children moving quickly to the cars—and he heard the thunder. If he read the same story in a book about another little boy, he wouldn't have the sensory clues to help him with the meaning.

Supporting English Language Learners: Retelling

- The experience happened to the students:
  - They can use sensory clues.
  - The meaning precedes the print.
  - The predictable structure of finding and practicing the story provides a scaffold.
- The words are provided:
  - They learn key phrases.
  - They use words in an authentic way.
  - They pronounce the words over and over.
- Story structure is modeled:
  - They hear correct sentence structure.
  - They retell the story aloud using correct sentence structure.

Figure 1.9 Supporting English Language Learners: Retelling

Choosing and Building a Class Story

O ur school staff meetings and teachers' lunchroom discussions buzz with stories about kids. We love to share the day's happenings with our coworkers. Told and retold, these stories become part of our school community. One of Connie's greatest hits is the story of the dead mole:

I couldn't imagine where the awful smell was coming from! I looked in every single desk. I threw out old sandwiches and tissues. I found some things I couldn't even identify—but that smell wouldn't go away. Then I noticed a jacket hanging on a hook in the back. The closer I got, the stronger the smell. The smell was coming from the coat. Then I put it all together! The day before, Dillon had given me a mole. Not a plastic mole, but a real dead mole. He had laid it across my desk, so proud to introduce me to his friend. I had casually mentioned the day before that I had never seen a real mole. Well, Dillon went out and found me one! When I'd asked him to get rid of it, I guess he simply put it in the pocket of his jacket and left it there!

Her all-ears listeners were late getting back to their classes from the lunchroom, and the story was retold many times that day. First grade heard it as an introduction to the concept of showing, not telling. For fourth graders it was a model for a twist ending.

Connie's class used it to practice sequential retelling. It became a staple in Connie's storytelling backpack.

We want our students to fill up their own storytelling backpacks. We want them to own the stories of their lives and use them to expand their literacy. While any number of stories happens every day in our classrooms, they can't all become springboards for practicing reading and writing skills. If there are particular skills and strategies we want to introduce and practice, we have to stock the story with those skills and strategies from the beginning.

Stories are flexible. Built and told differently, the mole story can show how sound words help listeners visualize the story or highlight the way transition words move a story along. Deliberate use of writer's craft makes a story a more powerful tool for bridging oral language with print. We also need to keep in mind district and state literacy standards; how do we fit all this in and make it replicable in other classrooms?

This chapter shares our process for ensuring that our class stories become effective mentor texts in our literacy units. Building stories that support our literacy curriculum requires thoughtful planning and deliberate insertion of the skills we want to highlight. Retelling these stories orally allows students to practice these skills and apply them in print in the future.

But first, stories need to be found!

Laying the Groundwork: Sharing Stories from Our Lives

We always begin the school year by encouraging students to find the stories of their lives and to write those stories down during writing workshop. We begin with the simple reminder that they all have stories to tell. This is more challenging for some students than for others. Gustavo puts his head down and says, "I don't have anything to write." Yaseen says that nothing ever happens where he lives. Emma tells the class that she only knows how to draw rainbows. Blake says he only knows how to draw dogs. Jo Jo cries because he can't draw a circle. Lilly says she never gets to go anywhere! Being explicit about how to recognize a story is the first step to help each student learn how to tell and how to write one.

We begin the first moments of the first day of school with a first-day story. Maybe Mrs. Dierking tells how she spent last night writing their names on their book baskets, excited about meeting each of them in person. Perhaps Mrs. Jones shares how she felt when she saw the shiny buses drive up to the school that morning, all pretty and clean. Then we share a personal story from our own lives, modeling not only how a story goes but also the idea that everyone has stories to tell: "I have a story to share with you. This is something that really happened to me, and this is how it goes. One time . . .".

We continue sharing stories during the first few weeks of school (and beyond), wherever they fit best: the first few minutes of the day, after a read-aloud, as the students line up to go to lunch, and just before dismissal. Any time we find a few extra minutes is a good time to share a story.

We don't share the big stories (the trip we took to Disney World), but small, everyday stories featuring our families, pets, or funny mishaps. Sherra tells how she lost her keys and her daughter found them in the refrigerator. Connie recalls the squirrels who built a nest in the ceiling of her kindergarten classroom. These stories allow our students to get to know us as mothers, as friends, and most important as their teachers.

Spending the first few weeks of school modeling how to share the stories of our lives makes a huge impact. Our students are captivated by our stories (and yours will be too). They often ask for their favorites to be repeated. Whetting their story appetite puts them on the edge of their seats. Sherra begins one of her favorites like this:

> Boys and girls, you will never believe what happened to me this morning on my way to work. I was driving through Dunkin' Donuts to buy a cup of coffee, when all of a sudden, a donut fell out of the sky and landed, THUD, right on the hood of my car. Would you like to hear the story about the time a donut fell out of the sky?

Naturally, her students are intrigued and insist that she go on with the story. Sherra holds her hand to her head, as if she's thinking she needs some time to remember how the story goes because she wants to be sure to tell it in the right order so it makes sense.

Students respect the fifteen or so seconds she spends pretending to run through the story in her head. They sit silently staring at this person who is about to entertain them with a story they are eager to hear:

I think I am ready to tell my story. Early this morning, I was driving through Dunkin' Donuts to buy myself a cup of coffee. All of a sudden, a donut fell out of the sky and landed, THUD, right on the hood of my car! The noise startled me so much that I jumped and hit the top of my head. At first, I was confused, but then I saw the seagull. It was circling around and around the front of my car. I sat very still and watched as that seagull swooped down and snatched that donut off my car with his beak! I figured he must have been flying over my car when he accidently dropped his breakfast. Now, every time I go to Dunkin' Donuts, I will remember that silly seagull.

Listening to us tell stories helps our students develop a sense of the way stories go. Awareness of story is a new concept for many of them. Immersion in oral stories is also an important first step in emergent reading and writing. Our demonstrations plant the idea that stories can grow out of any event and are meant to be shared. Our stories become living books students "check out" over and over. (Favorites in Sherra's classroom: "Learning That Roaches Can Fly," "Underwater Racing with My Daughter," "A Bee Flying Up My Dress," "My Dog Chasing an Egret," "Getting Gum Stuck in My Hair," and "Locking My Keys in the Car." Favorites in Connie's classroom: "Finding a Snake in the Mailbox," "Giving My Kitty a Bath," "When the Bulletin Board Fell Off the Wall," "Losing My Lunchbox," "Running Out of Gas," and "Dropping My Ice Cream Cone.")

As we tell stories of our own, we keep our eyes and ears open for shared classroom experiences that may become the oral stories—the oral mentor texts—of our curriculum. We tell our students that we are on the lookout for stories about events that happen right here at school. We reinforce that these shared events can be told as stories to other people. We remind them how interested their families are in hearing about the things that happen at school. These shared events are stories they can tell their moms, dads, grandmas, cousins, and so forth.

At first, it is mostly we who identify shared experiences as potential class stories, but soon our students want to be included in the quest. Once they catch on to the idea that any shared happening can be a story to tell, they are unstoppable! They take pride in being the first to notice that something the class experiences is a possible story topic.

The most important lesson we want our students to learn during the early days of school is that we are a community. As we spend many hours a day together, things will happen to us, events we can tell to others. We can practice retelling these events so that the stories are fun and interesting to listen to. We don't parrot a mundane set of sentences about finding a lizard in the wastebasket or a windstorm on the P.E. field. We get pumped up about retelling a shared experience as a "happening" others will want to hear retold over and over, like a favorite book! We are in the storytelling business, and our first order of business is to look for a shared story to tell.

As the year progresses, students become experts at finding the stories of their lives. They pay attention to their experiences and realize those experiences can become stories to share. They begin to see everything, from recess being canceled to a lizard in the boy's bathroom, as a potential story to tell.

Choosing or Orchestrating a Shared Experience

The first story of the year needs to capture an experience that can be sequenced and retold. The point is to retell an event so that it sounds like a tale from a book. Some of ours have been about things as simple as:

» Coming to the rug for writing workshop
» Getting a drink from the water fountain
» Locating the recycling bin
» Lining up for lunch
» The first fire drill
» A visit from the principal
» Checking out books from the library

These aren't the most exciting things to happen at school, but they are a great place to start: simple events every child has experienced, easily sequenced and told as a story.

We all occasionally need a nudge to get started. A fun alternative to choosing a story from the events that happen naturally in the classroom is to make something exciting happen that *all* children in the class experience. This can involve another teacher, the principal, a parent—anyone.

For example, every year Sherra's class practices fluency by reading from their poetry notebooks. On a day Sherra's students were going to read "Spaghetti, Spaghetti" (we use one stanza from the poem by Jack Prelutsky), she arranged for Connie and her students to burst into the classroom holding cups of spaghetti, chant "Mama Mia, Mama Mia," and recite "Spaghetti, Spaghetti." Sherra's students were amazed and delighted—and Sherra had a memorable, shared experience ready to be turned into an oral mentor text stocked with the skills she wanted her class to practice (including reciting the poem):

> BANG! BANG! BANG! "What in the world is that?" demanded Mrs. Jones. Before she could open the door, Mrs. Dierking's class barged in holding cups of spaghetti. They were chanting, "Mama Mia, Mama Mia." Then they read us a poem called "Spaghetti, Spaghetti" by Jack Prelutsky:
>
> > Spaghetti, spaghetti,
> > I love you a lot.
> > You're splishy, you're sploshy,
> > Delicious and hot!
> > I gobble you down,
> > Oh, I can't get enough.
> > Spaghetti, spaghetti,
> > You're wonderful stuff!
>
> "That's the same poem we were working on," cried Garrett. Before they left, they passed around the little cups of spaghetti. Elizabeth whispered, "That was as funny as a circus clown."

Other setups could center on dropping a fake bug, letting a shoe fly off the end of your foot, or pretending not to be able to find something. There's no right or wrong way to create a memorable, story-worthy experience. The beauty is, you know what is coming and can be prepared. You can even plan how many sentences to use to tell the story and what vocabulary to insert.

A story based on a prearranged happening can become an anchor story used year after year. It's designed to support language development at a particular point in the year and aligned with district or state standards. We caution, though, that the most effective class stories are based on an authentic class experience. Students need to see generating stories as part of living—any given moment may become a story to share.

Building the Story

After we identify the event that will become the shared story, we prepare how the story will go before we present it to the class: We write it down exactly how we want it to sound. It may seem strange not to ask the children to help compose the story, but we want to include specific components, such as dialogue, varied sentence structure, and precise words appropriate for these students. Students also need the opportunity to practice the skills and strategies appropriate to the unit of study we are teaching and district and state guidelines. If students help in the composition, the story too easily goes off track.

Our initial focus is on sequence—teaching students to retell what happened in the order it happened. We keep the sentence structure simple and include some dialogue (children love hearing their names, and dialogue is easy for them to remember). Here is a short list of guidelines for structuring the first class story:

> » Use seven to ten sentences.
> » Keep sentence structure simple, but use a variety of structures.
> » Include dialogue.
> » Include students' names.
> » Use precise language appropriate for your students' developmental level.

We struggled with whether students should see the story in print, and decided they shouldn't. We record the story in writing so we can repeat it the same way each time, but this written version is only for us. Instruction and practice is oral until students know the story so well that we can teach into it.

Building (writing) the class story doesn't take a long time, but we do it thoughtfully. The essential requirement is having a clear idea about what we want the story to teach. We build the story to support our instruction. For example, if several writing workshop minilessons deal with active verbs, we include some active verbs. If a reading workshop minilesson highlights the way a character changes during the course of a story, we compose a class story in which the main character changes (for example, Sarah screams when she sees the lizard in the trash can but finally helps take it outside). We control the vocabulary, structure, and craft. It is our job to include specific goals and teaching points that support our students' literacy development.

The narratives students encounter need to prompt an accurate expectation of how a story goes. The Common Core State Standards lay out the basic tenets of narrative structure in the "reading literature," "writing narrative," and "speaking and listening" standards. The stories students tell and write need to include a setting, characters, a plot, and a resolution. The story details are the "evidence" that supports meaning.

Our building blocks for composing a class story (see page 24) move from the general to the specific. We include skill and strategy practice. We also ensure that every story contains craft elements. We always include strong leads and endings, dialogue, varied sentence structures, precise verbs, appropriate grammar, and rich vocabulary.

Steps in Building a Shared Class Narrative

» Identify the standards that support your learning goal for reading or writing.
» List the reading, writing, language, and/or speaking and listening skills you will teach for the month (or unit of study).
» Highlight the skills and strategies you want to include.
» Choose craft considerations.
» Build a story that includes these skills, strategies, and craft considerations.

Identifying the Standards

We begin by identifying the Common Core State Standards or state benchmarks that will guide our instruction. One or more of these standards become our learning goal—the literacy outcome we are seeking in reading, writing, speaking, and listening. We build our class story so that repeated retellings will help our students reach this goal.

For example, one of Connie's third-grade units of study is narrative. She finds the standards that address narrative reading and writing and identifies one or two as learning goals. The standards become her framework for teaching the narrative unit—things she may include in the class story. She examines the standards for writing and language and highlights those that would support her reading instruction. Finally, she highlights the speaking and listening standards that would support the literacy goals for the unit.

Common Core State Standards for Reading Literature

» RL.3.1—Ask and answer questions to demonstrate understanding of a text, referring explicitly to the text as the basis for the answers.
» RL.2.3—Describe how characters respond to major events and challenges.
» RL.2.5—Describe the overall structure of a story, including how the beginning introduces the story and the ending concludes the action.
» RF.3.4—Read with sufficient accuracy and fluency to support comprehension.

Common Core State Standards for Writing and Language

» W.3.3a, b, c, d—Write narratives to develop real or imagined experiences or events using effective technique, descriptive details, and clear event sequences.

» L.3.1—Demonstrate command of the conventions of standard English grammar and usage when writing or speaking.

» L.3.4a—Use sentence-level context as a clue to the meaning of a word or phrase.

Common Core State Standards for Speaking and Listening

» SL.3.2—Determine the main ideas and supporting details of a text read aloud or information presented in diverse media and formats, including visually, quantitatively, and orally.

» SL.3.4—Report on a topic or text, tell a story, or recount an experience with appropriate facts and relevant, descriptive details, speaking clearly at an understandable pace.

Once she has standards in mind she is ready to think about specifics for the class story. While she may only use one standard as the foundation for her class story, highlighting all those that pertain to the unit gives her the big picture.

List the Reading, Writing, Language, and/or Speaking and Listening Skills You Will Teach for the Month (or Unit of Study)

Teaching points are the specifics of a lesson, the skills that lead to mastering the larger standards. When planning a unit (or preparing to teach a unit that has been provided by the district or a professional resource) we must decide which skills are appropriate for our class and which ones we want to include in the class story. Once we decide, we can build the story using the words, sentences, and paragraphs that provide the necessary practice.

Here are the reading and writing skills Connie considers as she builds her story. She has many choices; the good news is that whichever ones she includes will support her learning goal.

Reading and Writing Skills Connie's Students Could Practice Using the Class Story

Reading Skills

» *Using evidence from the text to answer question about events.*
She could include details that a story listener would need to answer questions about the event in the story.

» *Finding evidence in the text that defines how characters respond to events in the text.*
She could make a character in the story respond to something in the story.

» *Identifying the text structure as opinion, explanatory, or narrative.*
She could include all the elements of narrative.

» *Using one's voice to distinguish among characters.*
She could include dialogue.

» *Retelling the story using facts and details from the text.*
She could include sensory details.

» *Using punctuation in the text.*
The class could practice stopping at the ends of sentences to take a breath when reciting the story.

Writing Skills

» *Including a sequence of events to retell a story.*
She will include a sequence of events.

» *Using descriptive details to help the reader visualize.*
She could use descriptive details in the story.

» *Using temporal words to move the story along.*
She could use temporal words.

» *Writing with punctuation in order to help the reader.*
The class could practice the punctuation of the class story by writing in the air.

Highlight the Skills You Want to Include in Your Shared Class Narrative

We use all the previous information as we craft our class story. We want it to provide deliberate practice toward our reading and/or writing goal. Figure 2.1 shows how Connie decided to stock the oral class story that follows. Connie chose to include

CCSS	Reading Skills	Writing Skill	Include in Class Story
Anchor Standard 5: Analyze the structure of texts, including how specific sentences, paragraphs, and larger portions of the text relate to each other and the whole.	• Identifying the text structure as opinion, explanatory, or narrative • Retelling the story using facts and details from the text	• Including a sequence of events to retell a story	• Strong setting • Specific events told in order • Beginning that introduces the story line

Figure 2.1 Considerations for Stocking the Oral Shared Story

these particular skills based on the needs of her students; you will highlight skills based on the needs of yours.

Connie's Stocked Oral Shared Story

> It was a hot, humid afternoon as we hunched over our writing. The vibrating hum of the lawnmower rattled the windows like a storm. *[Descriptive details, introduces suspense]* Suddenly, BAM, BOOM, BAM, the entire wall shook in our classroom. *[Strong setting, temporal words, sequence of events]* We jerked our heads up in time to see the map on the wall teetering on a small hook. It moved slowly, back and forth, back and forth. Squeak, squeak, squeak, clank. The map dropped slowly to the floor, unfolding crookedly. *[Details]* "What just happened?" laughed our teacher, Mrs. Dierking. "It was like slow motion!" said Marianna. "I bet it was the rattling from the lawn mower!" replied Blake. "Or maybe a ghost who doesn't like geography!" teased Carrie. *[Dialogue, text evidence to support opinion, sequence of events]*

We use certain craft elements in all our oral stories as well. Strong leads help students remember how their story begins. (Sounds familiar, right?) Stories that include dialogue with student names as speaker tags generate excitement and provide superb practice in intonation and prosody. To model correct structure and grammar, we include a variety of sentence types. We also include strong verbs to counteract wimpy words like *nice* and *fun*. Many other craft elements also provide "bang for your buck." While we haven't identified them as "musts," they are worth including in later class stories. As goals and teaching points become more sophisticated, oral stories should as well. (Detailed explanations of all craft considerations are presented in Chapters 4 and 5.)

Craft Elements to Include in All Class Stories
» Strong leads
  ○ Weather
  ○ Sound
  ○ Quotation
  ○ Feeling
  ○ Hint

» Strong endings
  ○ Circular
  ○ Feeling
  ○ Question
  ○ Twist
» Dialogue
  ○ Student speaker tags
  ○ Teacher speaker tags
» Temporal words
» Varied sentences
» Precise verbs
» Appropriate grammar and usage
  ○ Proper nouns
  ○ Subject-verb agreement
  ○ Possessives
» Rich vocabulary

Expanding Class Stories Throughout the Year

Because the oral story is a vehicle for practicing oral language and literacy skills either previously introduced or to be introduced, the language changes from story to story. Students are introduced to a variety of written text types and genres throughout the year, and oral stories must reflect that variety. The length and complexity of each successive story should match the increased sophistication in reading and writing proficiency throughout the year. Retelling an oral story using transition words would not accelerate literacy growth in the spring of third grade; if the story needs to be more complex, use more sophisticated transitions between events.

We identify the teaching standards and skills for the month or unit, but we also consider the language development of our students. We wouldn't include multiple compound sentences in kindergarten. The structure of our sentences resembles the expressive language of our students. It may take several attempts before the story captures the experience, sounds authentic, and includes relevant skills. Also, we don't need to include everything in one story because we have an entire year's worth of stories to stock with helpful skills and strategies.

Building a class story is no different from planning any other literacy instruction. Keeping our particular students in mind, we identify standards and our learning goal, choose teaching points and skills that will lead students to that goal, and find the materials to help us. The beauty of the class story is that we build the material (the story) to provide the exact practice students need. The class story is the "just right" scaffold for reaching identified literacy goals. Once you've stocked a few stories, the process will become more fluid and organic; you'll have the standards and teaching points in mind, and you'll know what skills you want to include in the story as you write it. Examples of finding, planning, and building a first-grade and a third-grade class story are provided next.

Finding, Planning, and Building a First-Grade Class Story

Shared Experience	CCSS	Reading Skills	Writing Skills	Stocked Oral Story
Storm moving in on the first day of school	RL.1.1.2—Retell stories including key details, and demonstrate understanding of their central message or lesson. RL.1.3.7—Use illustrations and details in a story to describe its characters, setting, or events. W.1.1.3—Write narratives in which they recount two or more appropriately sequenced events; include some details regarding what happened; use temporal words to signal event order; and provide some sense of closure. SL.1.2.4—Describe people, places, things, and events with relevant details, expressing ideas and feelings clearly.	• Beginning–middle–end. • Identifying the setting. • Retelling. • Naming the characters. • Visualizing. • Understanding the author's message.	• Beginning–middle–end. • Using temporal words. • Using description. • Matching illustrations with the words.	Yesterday was the first day of school. At the end of the day, we had art with Mr. Prankard. Just before 2:00, Mrs. Jones picked us up. "Hurry," she warned, "it's about to rain." As we walked to the car line, we noticed the gray clouds in the sky. The thunder rumbled. We wondered if we would make it to our cars before the storm.

Finding, Planning, and Building a Third-Grade Class Story

Shared Experience	CCSS	Reading Skills	Writing Skills	Stocked Oral Story
Map falling off the wall	RL.3.2–Recount stories, including fables, folktales, and myths, and determine the central message, lesson, or moral, and explain how it is conveyed through key details in the text. RL.3.8–Distinguish their own point of view from that of the narrator or those of the characters. W.3.3–Write narratives to develop real or imagined experiences of events using effective technique, descriptive details, and clear event sequences. SL.3.4–Report on a topic or text, tell a story, or recount an experience with appropriate facts and relevant descriptive details, speaking clearly at an understandable pace.	• Retelling. • Identifying using descriptive details. • Expressing point of view. • Using text evidence to support an opinion.	• Naming a topic. • Building suspense. • Showing support through details. • Using sound words. • Using temporal words. • Using dialogue.	It was a hot, humid afternoon as we hunched over our writing. The vibrating hum of the lawnmower rattled the windows like a storm. Suddenly, BAM, BOOM, BAM, the entire wall shook in our classroom. We jerked our heads up in time to see the map on the wall teetering on a small hook. It moved slowly, back and forth, back and forth. Squeak, squeak, squeak, clank. The map dropped slowly to the floor, unfolding crookedly. "What just happened?" laughed our teacher, Mrs. Dierking. "It was like slow motion!" said Marianna. "I bet it was the rattling from the lawn mower!" replied Blake. "Or maybe a ghost who doesn't like geography!" teased Carrie.

CHAPTER 3

Learning and Practicing the Class Story

nyone spending time around a child just learning language has witnessed the power of practice. The word *mama* or *doggie* rolls off a baby's tongue only after many repetitions. The class story has to be told and retold before it is internalized. For the story to succeed as a mentor oral text, children have to be able to retrieve it from their long-term memory on demand as a reference during reading and writing.

When we began our work with class stories, we pondered this idea of practice. How did we want it to look? How did we want it to sound? How would we keep students engaged? Gradually, a list of considerations specific to practice emerged:

» Students should be eager to practice their class stories; the work should be engaging.
» They should incorporate symbols and gestures to help them retrieve words.
» They should tell longer and more sophisticated stories as the year progresses.
» They should retell stories with accuracy.
» They should pay attention to phrasing and expression.
» They should use an appropriate rate.
» Every child should be able to participate successfully.
» The class story should help children practice conventions in the air.
» Students should use a strong, clear voice and make eye contact with their audience.
» There should be opportunities throughout the day to practice telling the story as a class.

For students to be able to make authentic connections, the entire class must practice telling the story every day. The school day already bulges at the seams with everything we are required to do. The beauty of practicing the class story is that it can be done quickly, at any time once the story has been introduced. We practice it while the class walks to the lunchroom. Five minutes between lunch and art? Waiting for the media specialist? We practice the class story.

However, rote memorization isn't the way to go because students' desire to learn the story evaporates. To spice it up a bit, to keep the story fresh, we use varied structures for practicing the story. A very important goal is for students to tell the story accurately, at a "just right" rate, paying attention to phrasing and expression. As a conductor teaching a new piece to his orchestra highlights each instrument, we highlight each student. We want every student to feel a part of the story. We make sure our students understand that the story grew out of an event at which each one of them was present. Likewise, the story must be told by each one of them. Nonparticipation is not an option. We are all in the class story together. And students support one another in touching ways. During one story practice, Chloe whispered to Daniella, "You can watch my mouth if you need to!" Practicing the class story builds community.

Paying close attention to detail is imperative during the beginning stages. We highlight proper enunciation and phrasing. Because everything is practiced "in the air," students can concentrate fully on how their oral presentation sounds. Because we have built the story so that students practice what we deem important, it is easy to listen for these skills and strategies.

Reading coach Allison Sisco was the impetus for a class story in Amy Owens's first-grade classroom when, dressed up as a spider princess for Halloween, her eye fell out:

On Halloween we went to hear a story in Mrs. Sisco's office. She was dressed up as a spider princess. After the story, we lined up to leave. But Mrs. Sisco had something wrong with her. All of a sudden, her eye fell on the floor. Everyone screamed. Michael picked it up, "Eww, it is slimy!" Devonte said, "I think I am going to faint." Mrs. Sisco laughed, "Trick or treat!" The eye was the trick but then she gave us rings and spiders for a treat. We never know what Mrs. Sisco is going to do next!

As Amy's class began learning the story, it was important to get several phrases right. Her students were repeating, "Everyone screamed. Michael picked it up. 'Eww, it is slimy!' Devonte said. 'I think . . . .' "

That isn't how the story went: *Michael* said, "Eww, it is slimy." The students quickly realized that if they repeated the story without the correct phrasing it sounded like Devonte did all the talking. This kind of attention to phrasing is very clear when retelling a story in which all the students are participants.

Symbols and gestures are also important elements of practicing oral class stories. Symbols (as simple as a triangle or as sophisticated as a drawing of a person) support the story visually. They help students understand elements of the story and support retelling. Gestures that match actions in the story are also helpful. (Our students think they're the best part!) Early on, they hold the story together. It's natural to use our hands when speaking: Gestures help us get a point across, emphasize what is important, and add flair to everyday conversations. Fitting actions to the words helps students hold on to meaning and retrieve words. When, as a class, we invent gestures to go with an action, our students are full of ideas. They've created animals with their body, twirled their fingers to represent the wind, and given arm pumps to show the sky's the limit! (We have to rein in our enthusiastic storytellers if the gestures become too complicated.) The only rule for creating a gesture is that it must help the storyteller remember how that part of the story goes.

We practice each story every day, in some way, for approximately four weeks. This keeps the story on the tip of each student's tongue until it becomes a permanent part of their working memory. As we mentioned, brief practices can be slipped into odd moments of free time. Some teachers designate a specific time of the day. Before morning announcements works well, as does the end of the day after packing up to go home. Connie sometimes starts her reading block by practicing the class story.

The initial instruction in how to practice the story can take fifteen or twenty minutes, but once students learn the structures, practice sessions only take a minute or two. A story won't be internalized in a day or even a week, but the payback once it has been is worth it.

Structures for Learning a Class Story

We use four "story-starting" strategies to help students learn and begin telling the class story:

1. Echo telling
2. Adding symbols
3. Adding gestures
4. Choral telling

We begin with echo telling. Symbols and gestures provide support later as the class moves toward telling the story chorally. Since symbols and gestures serve the same purpose—helping students retrieve words—the order in which they are introduced doesn't matter. However, with kindergartners we introduce the story, have them echo tell it, then add gestures, then add symbols, and finally tell the story in unison. With first through third graders, one or more strategies can be used at the same time.

Echo Telling

We introduce each new class story by telling the story ourselves so students hear how it sounds. The next step is echo telling: We say one sentence at a time, using the appropriate phrasing and intonation, and the students echo that sentence back until the story is completed:

> **Teacher:** Have you ever heard that two heads are better than one?
> **Students:** Have you ever heard that two heads are better than one?
> **Teacher:** Well, we think two teachers are better than one.
> **Students:** Well, we think two teachers are better than one.

Having students echo each sentence provides very strong support—we can highlight any tricky words or phrases. Our goal is to help students commit the story to memory so they can tell it accurately, in the correct sequence. Students mimic our cadence, phrasing, and expression, so we are thoughtful about how we sound.

It's easy to echo tell the story several times a day; it takes only a few minutes and can be slid in anywhere. There is no right amount of time to spend on this step. Some stories are easier to commit to memory than others, and the length of time also depends on your class and grade level.

Adding Symbols

Once students are very familiar with the story, we add symbols—little pictures that stand for a word, phrase, or sentence. For example, a red shape with eight sides stands for *stop*. It need not include the word *stop* (although it often does); rather, it is a symbol for *stop*. Having each sentence of the story represented by a symbol makes it easier for students to retrieve the words that tell the story. These visual aids also help children sequence the story accurately.

Symbols need to be meaningful for students, so we ask them to help create them. We gather students in front of a piece of chart paper or a white board divided into as many boxes as there are sentences in the story. We say the first line of the story, and as a class (or individually or with a partner) brainstorm a symbol that will represent what the sentence says and help students remember it.

For example, if the first line of her class story is *On our way to lunch, we stopped to look at the butterfly garden*, Sherra might say, "Boys and girls, think of a symbol that will help us remember to say that sentence," and then ask them to turn and talk with a partner while she listens to their ideas. Then she might say, "Boys and girls, I was listening as you shared your ideas. I heard a lot of people saying that we should use a butterfly. That makes sense to me, because it would help us remember to say that we stopped at the butterfly garden. I also heard a few people saying that we should use a lunch box. That makes sense to me too, because we were on our way to lunch. I'm going to use both of those symbols to help us remember how to start our class story." Then Sherra draws a lunch box and a butterfly in the top left box of the chart paper and points to these symbols as she asks students to say the first line of the story. "Boys and girls, do you see how we did that? We thought of two symbols that would help us remember how the story starts. We can do that for each sentence in the story." (Examples of symbol grids are shown in Figures 3.1 and 3.2.)

Visual representation using symbols is nothing new. Authors have been story-boarding for ages! Explicitly teaching students to apply symbols to thoughts that go together to make a story helps the story stick.

Adding symbols can take several days or be accomplished quickly in one sitting. It depends on the grade level of the students, the number of ELL learners in the class, and how complicated the story is.

Telling the class story many times using the symbols helps students retrieve the right words in the right order. We sometimes create small individual copies of the symbols that students can use for independent practice. Often the symbols are enough of a scaffold that we can jump directly to choral telling.

BANG! BANG! BANG! "What in the world is that," demanded Mrs. Jones. Before she could open the door, Mrs. Dierking's class barged in holding little cups of spaghetti. They were all chanting, "Mama Mia, Mama Mia." Then they read us a poem called "Spaghetti, Spaghetti."

Spaghetti, spaghetti,
I love you a lot.
You're splishy, you're sploshy,
Delicious and hot!
I gobble you down,
Oh, I can't get enough.
Spaghetti, spaghetti,
You're wonderful stuff!

"That's the same poem we were working on," cried Garrett. Before they left, they passed around the little cups of spaghetti. Elizabeth whispered, "That was as funny as a circus clown."

Figure 3.1 Symbol Grid for the "Spaghetti, Spaghetti" Story

We were just finishing math when we heard a knock, a knock, a knock upon the door. It was Mrs. Noordhoek!

"Miss Bakewell, when is your class going outside to play?" she asked. "As soon as we put away our math tubs," said Miss Bakewell.

"Hurry, hurry, clean up speedy quick," said Mrs. Noordhoek. "I want to go on the swings with you."

So we put away our supplies as quick as a wink and lined up quietly. Shh, shh, we lined up quietly.

When we got outside Mrs. Noordhoek raced to the swings and was the first to jump on.

We couldn't believe how high she went. A way up high and a way down low.

We had fun with Mrs. Noordhoek.

I wonder if she'll come back and swing with us again. Hmm, I wonder.

Figure 3.2 Symbol Grid for "Fun with Mrs. Noordhoek"

Using Gestures

Through gestures, we interact with language physically. Most people talk with their hands. It's natural to put a hand out into the air when saying *stop*, for example. Gestures, in particular, support kinesthetic learners. Attaching movement to words helps the words stick and increases engagement with the class story.

We explain that we want to make our class story interactive and ask students to suggest gestures to go along with the words. This also helps us identify which students understand it. One of Connie's class stories began, *Ring! Ring! We rushed to the door as the fire alarm pierced our ears!* When Jaen suggested that a helpful gesture would be to "point to your finger," Connie knew he didn't understand the correct meaning of the word *ring*. He'd heard the fire alarm go off, but being new to English, he knew only one meaning for the word *ring*.

For gestures to be meaningful, students need to understand the connection between the words in a sentence and the accompanying gesture. Playing charades can prepare students for how to add gestures and show them how movement helps us interpret language. We both use gestures when we teach new vocabulary words, and these gestures crop up naturally when students recite the class story (see Figure 3.3).

Here's how Sherra might create a gesture to accompany *on our way to lunch, we stopped to look at the butterfly garden*:

> Boys and girls, turn and talk to your partner about a hand movement that would help us remember this line. *[She listens in and then shares their smart ideas.]* I noticed that many of you were fluttering your arms like a butterfly would flutter its wings. That makes sense, because we want to remember to say that we stopped at the butterfly garden. Let's use that gesture to help us remember how to start the story.

Once gestures have been generated and practiced, the students use both the symbols and the gestures to retell the story many times, after which they are ready to move on.

Choral Telling

The final step in getting the oral class story up and running is choral telling. Choral telling allows students to practice whatever parts of the story they know, even if it's just reciting a word here or there, without feeling that they are being put on the spot. However, the goal is for all students to be able to tell the entire story as one voice. Every student uses the symbols and gestures to tell the story at the same rate, with the

Figure 3.3 Kindergartners use gestures to retell their story.

same cadence, phrasing, and expression. Everyone shines because everyone knows the story!

We seize every opportunity to choral tell—in the classroom and outside of it. The few minutes it takes are well worth the time.

Structures for Practicing a Class Story

Once we have found, built, and taught the class story, the fun begins! We practice the story until students can call it up and use it to recognize skills and strategies. To internalize a class story to that degree, students have to practice—a lot.

We both were active in theatre in high school, and it stuck. We know how important it is to speak to the back of the room, repeat lines over and over, change phrasing, and punch particular words for effect. When children perform an oral class story, they experience the craft of composition *and* the thrill of performing their composition. Practicing helps them make their oral presentation the very best it can be: performance ready.

To keep students excited and engaged, we developed six ways to practice. No structure trumps the others; they are all effective. Once students are able to use these techniques proficiently, they choose their favorite(s) to retell their own stories during literacy centers, as homework, or in reading or writing workshop. (See more about that in Chapters 4 and 5.)

Structures for Practicing a Class Story

» Get good at telling one sentence/incident at a time.
» Tell it in a circle.
» Use popcorn telling.
» Tell it like a book.
» Tell it to a partner.
» Tell it to an audience.

Get Good at Telling One Sentence/Incident

Students who struggle with expressive language or feel uncomfortable speaking in front of peers usually choose to blend in with the crowd. They mumble along or yell out the words they know. By practicing one sentence over and over, these students gain fluency and confidence, are eager to move on to another sentence and then another, and are eventually able to tell the entire story with fluency and excitement.

First, we divide the oral story into sentences (in kindergarten and first grade) or incidents (which can be several sentences). Then we give each sentence or incident a number. (For example, in "Spaghetti, Spaghetti," *BANG! BANG! BANG! "What in the world is that," demanded Mrs. Jones* is number 1. *Before she could open the door, Mrs. Dierking's class barged in holding little cups of spaghetti* is number 2.) We write the numbers on 8½ × 11 sheets of paper and place them around the room. Students stand next to the number of the sentence/incident they want to practice (see Figure 3.4). When we practice the story, only the students standing next to the corresponding number tell that sentence/incident orally.

Sometimes students practice the same sentence/incident in all retellings during a given day. The next day they might switch (or not). Some days we have "fruit basket upset," and students switch sentences/incidents after each retelling. If students need the added scaffold of a symbol pasted on the number, we provide it.

Figure 3.4 Third graders practice getting good at a page.

Tell It in a Circle

Because oral storytelling is a community event, telling the story in a circle makes a lot of sense. A group of students forms a circle, and one student begins the story. The next person in the circle tells the next sentence/incident, and so on until the end. Then the next person begins the story again. This continues until every student has participated (see Figure 3.5).

The circle structure allows students to see one another and encourages the use of gestures. For example, when Connie was a reading coach, a kindergarten class found a snake skin, an experience they used to create an oral class story:

> One day we were eating lunch in the garden. Zachary spied a snake skin in the bushes. Zachary yelled, "Look what I found!" Everyone stopped eating and ran over to look. Tatyanna said, "Ahhh, what is that?" The snake skin was brown, clear, and longer than a stick. Mrs. Craig put it in a container. Bella and Zachary carried it to our classroom. We still look at it every day.

Figure 3.5 Third graders practice the class story in a circle.

The class decided that, during the circle telling, whoever told the sentence in which Zachary yells, "Look what I found!" would hold up the container with the snake in it!

Use Popcorn Telling

Popcorn telling is a variation of circle telling. We select a student to start the story by gently tapping her or him on the shoulder. That student "pops up," tells the first sentence in the story, and taps another student (anyone in the circle) to continue the story (see Figure 3.6). When the story is finished, the next person tapped starts the story again. Students quickly realize they must follow the story closely so they'll know which sentence to share if they are tapped. The physicality of popping up keeps the students engaged and active.

This structure shouldn't be taught until students know the story fairly well. They have to stay focused, listen carefully to the sequence, and physically change their body position before and after reciting. They can help one another if a sentence is forgotten

Figure 3.6 First graders practice popcorn telling.

or words are left out. The goal is for the story to flow smoothly even though it is being told by random tellers.

Tell It Like a Book

Students need to understand the importance of sequence. Although representing the sentences/incidents numerically helps, it is also true that printed books are organized by pages turned as readers work their way through the story. At first we asked students to hold their hands in front of them like a little book and pretend to turn a page after each sentence/incident. They enjoyed this so much we now have them turn their entire bodies.

Here's how it works. Selecting as many students as there are sentences in the story, standing in order from left to right, tell one sentence at a time. When finished, each student turns his or her back to demonstrate physically that this part of the story has been presented and it's time for the next sentence (see Figure 3.7).

Figure 3.7 First graders turn the pages of their class story.

Tell It to a Partner

Telling the oral story to a partner allows students to tell the entire story independently but with support. The partners practice the class story any way they choose. Many alternate sentences/incidents. Some prefer to retell the whole story one at a time. Some move from number to number as they retell the story. Others sit in front of the easel displaying the symbol grid and tell the story in unison. We have had partners create their own symbol grid with sticky notes to prompt their retelling. The important thing is that both partners participate.

Partners choose an area in the room to practice the story together, depending on the method they want to use. (If they want to put numbered pieces of paper on the floor and move from one to the next as they retell the story, they need an area large enough to do that.) Sprinkled throughout the room, students work side by side to retell the class story with phrasing and enthusiasm (see Figure 3.8).

Figure 3.8 First-grade partners retell the class story.

Tell It to an Audience

As students develop their oral class stories, they need opportunities to share these stories with others. Many times students diligently create a story, but when given the opportunity to share their work orally they are unable to do so. They speak so quietly the audience can't hear a word; they struggle with fluency; they retell the story with no expression.

Practicing retelling in front of an audience is an important aspect of learning. It's a rehearsal for the celebratory final performance. Telling the story to someone else, students must speak loudly with diction and fluency. Audience feedback reinforces the work required to be ready for performance. Students also experience how excited others are to hear their stories. (Our students are proud to be known as "that class who tells the stories"!)

CCSS Connections

The Common Core State Standards emphasize how important it is for children to be able to speak audibly, in complete sentences, and provide detail when requested. The standards also call out the importance of knowing how to tell a story with descriptive details, speaking clearly at an understandable pace. The oral class story ensures that all students practice these skills. The final performance provides a meaningful assessment of these standards.

Students first tell the class story to an audience in the classroom. Standing or sitting next to their partner, they tell the story in unison. We invite the custodian, a media specialist, the reading coach—anyone willing to pop into our classroom and listen. This audience of one gives powerful, constructive feedback. (We have paper and pencil ready so he or she can take notes, and we have the feedback in writing.) Later we may take our students to another classroom, where they line up and retell the story using symbols and gestures. We have taken digital videos of students as they retell the story on a stage and have shared the performance on our in-school network and/or attached it to an electronic parent newsletter.

Every third-grade reading or writing celebration begins with telling an earlier class story. Students have fun reviewing previous class stories and marvel at how well they remember them. One year, Sherra centered her entire end-of-year celebration around her class stories. Parents and community members heard all the stories, which were bridged by student narrators. The stories highlighted a year of learning; students shared not only the stories but also how the stories helped them develop their literacy learning.

An Example of Effective Feedback

One of our colleagues, fourth-grade teacher Maria DeWese, has developed a process for offering feedback to our students. First, she makes sure we and our students understand how much she values storytelling by giving us an open invitation to her classroom. As soon as we walk through the door, her students move to their desks and take out sticky notes and pencils. As they listen to the story, they jot down specific feedback to offer their storytelling buddies. (Maria models this process for her students until they are every bit as good at it as she is.)

Some of their feedback is aimed at performance: *everyone knew the story so well, you sounded like one voice; you told the story with so much expression; your rate was perfect—not too fast and not too slow; everyone's eyes were on the audience.*

Other feedback is aimed at composition and craft. Maria never misses an opportunity to make connections between storytelling and story writing. She continually links the two, so her students are inspired to take to print the skills and strategies they are hearing orally. They notice and identify specific craft choices and connect those choices to their own work as writers:

> I like the way you used alliteration in your story—"pumpkin project day was practically perfect." I use alliteration when I write stories.

> I love the way you started your story with a sound lead, "drip-drop, drip-drop." I think I will try that in the next story I write.

> I noticed you used dialogue in your story several times. I do that when I write because I want to give the reader the sense of being right there in the story.

Then we reciprocate! Maria and her fourth graders have an open invitation to read their stories to our classes. Our students listen for craft similarities and offer specific feedback. They also offer feedback aimed at performance. It is a win-win situation for everyone. Any audience that values storytelling and applauds your students' efforts is a good audience.

Celebrating the Class Story

Celebrating the class story not only shows respect for a job well done but also lets us close down one story before we start another. A celebration is a signal that this story is ready to be used as a mentor text or in a literacy center, and that we need to be on the lookout for another shared experience that will become the next class story. However, we made sure our students realize that the story we are celebrating is not gone forever. Old familiar stories are always pulled back out and enjoyed. They are also used as mentor texts to teach comprehension.

A class story can be celebrated in any number of ways. We celebrate the end of each class story differently. We also let our students contribute celebration ideas. Sometimes a celebration is unique to a specific story. For example, Sherra's "Pumpkin Project Day" class story captured the time the whole class went to the cafeteria to carve pumpkins. When they were ready to celebrate the story, the students wanted to bake pumpkin pies, so Sherra integrated that celebration into her curriculum. First, they found a recipe on the Internet. Then they wrote a persuasive letter to the cafeteria manager convincing her to let them use the oven. Next, they made a list of the ingredients needed. While mixing the ingredients, they used measurement skills learned in math. When the pies were ready, they invited the principal and office staff to hear their final performance of the story and help them eat the pies.

All celebrations don't need to be lofty, involved projects, however. Once, Connie's class told how they went out in the courtyard and blew bubbles. When they were ready to celebrate this story, they decided to return to the courtyard and videotape themselves telling the story while a few students blew bubbles. They shared their video on our school's "TV network." (Our media specialist is always willing to highlight a class story.)

Nor do celebrations have to be specific to the story. Below we list a number of celebration ideas. Remember: It's not important *how* you celebrate, it's important *that* you celebrate.

Class Story Celebration Ideas

» **Publish the class story.** You send it off into the world, as you would a written story. Including the class story in the morning announcements heard and/or seen by the entire school makes students feel like celebrities!

» **Bake a cake.** Make a cake with your class to celebrate the "birth" of a class story. Then have a birthday party to enjoy your cake.

» **Have a popcorn party.** This is especially appropriate after you have taught students how to "popcorn tell" a story (practice structure 5).

» **Make wordless books.** Invite every student to create illustrations that go along with each incident in the class story. Have each student create a book cover and staple the illustrations together, in order, and share the book with a buddy in another class. Everyone tells the class story using her or his own wordless book.

» **Have a pajama party.** Your students have worked diligently to find, learn, and practice a class story, so celebrate with "a day of rest." Have students come to school in their pajamas and bring their favorite stuffed animal. Plan a few fun activities: special games, a movie, blowing bubbles, anything that says "we've earned a little down time."

» **Plan a special activity during recess.** This is especially nice if your students don't usually all play together. Use it as a reward for successfully learning and sharing a class story. Bonus: It's a great source for a class story!

» **Tell stories in the dark.** Invite each student to bring a flashlight to school and come prepared to tell a story from their life. Or they can retell favorite class stories. Schedule a time when they can sit in the dark and tell their stories.

» **Make a video of the class story.** Children love to hear and watch themselves on video. Record the story you are celebrating, along with a few old favorites. Then view it while enjoying a special snack. It's like going to a movie!

» **Have a storytelling festival** (with or without refreshments). You decide the structure. Limit the stories to class stories or include personal narratives. Have stories told by the whole class, small groups, partners, or individuals. Display wordless books. This celebration is most effective near the end of the year, when students can retell all their stories. Parents are sure to be impressed.

» **Create props or puppets to retell the story.** Imagine how engaged your students will be using their creativity to make props and puppets in the literacy center!

» **Illustrate the story and publish the illustrations on a bulletin board.** The bulletin board can be in your classroom or in a more public venue, such as the front office or the main entrance. Students feel pride in their accomplishment when their work is on display.

» **Offer to perform the story at a PTA meeting, volunteer breakfast, or any other schoolwide function.** Administrators love this because it shows parents and volunteers what's happening in the classroom.

» **Allow students to enter the class story onto a computer file.** Technology natives leap at any opportunity to use a computer. Use their eagerness to your advantage.

Making the Home Connection

It's important to connect classroom language work with students' home lives. Oral storytelling is an especially effective way to do so. Students are proud of their ability to tell stories that are fun and interesting for their family members to hear. Parents are delighted to listen to their child's stories. There is no better audience. Here are some effective strategies for making this connection:

» **Provide parent training.** At the beginning of the year, offer parents the opportunity to attend training that outlines the oral storytelling work that will be happening in your classroom. This helps parents see the connection between oral language and literacy. If they understand why their students are finding, building, practicing, and performing stories, they will more likely be active participants. Informed parents are better able to help their children look for and learn new stories. They are also better equipped to help with homework centered around storytelling.

» **Assign related homework.** Once a story is practiced and is performance ready, students will be eager to present the story to family members. Figure 3.9 shows a

Dear Parents,

Since the beginning of school, we have been working to develop our storytelling skills. Storytelling is an effective building block to literacy. Children who are effective storytellers are more likely to be successful readers and writers.

Please help your child celebrate our class story by finding at least five people that will listen to the story. Your child may use the attached symbol sheet to help him or her remember how the story goes. Fill out the recording sheet at the bottom of this letter and return it to school on Thursday. We will celebrate as a class when all sheets are returned.

Here are some helpful hints for offering positive feedback to your storyteller:

- I love the way you started your story with _____.
- _____ is such a great word. It's much better than saying _____.
- Using symbols to help you tell the story in order is so smart.
- You have such expression in your voice. It makes me want to pay attention.
- It's great how you used gestures to help you remember how the story goes.
- I noticed that you made people talk in your story.
- Your story was easy to listen to because you didn't tell it too fast or too slow.
- Your voice was loud and clear.
- You looked right at me when you were telling the story.

Thank You,

* *

Child's Name: _____

Five people that listened to me tell our class story:

1. _____

2. _____

3. _____

4. _____

5. _____

Figure 3.9 Sample Parent Letter

generic letter that will help parents offer positive feedback and encouragement to their young storytellers.

» **Feature class stories during parent /teacher conferences.** If you have access to a digital video camera, tape each child performing a story and share the video at a parent/teacher conference. Many parents tear up at the sight of their child telling a story accurately and with expression.

» **Hold a storytelling festival for parents.** Students can tell stories as a class, with a partner, and/or individually. Having several parents tell their own stories (the time Sarah fell off her bike and had to get stitches, or the time Johnny cut his own hair) makes the celebration really special.

However you decide to include parents in oral storytelling, the process will be beneficial. Parents and students alike enjoy any homework or activity that involves storytelling. Parents have been eager, helpful participants in our endeavor to teach children how to tell stories with confidence and enthusiasm.

Relevant Common Core State Standards Across Grades

Reading Standards for Literature

Kindergarten	First Grade	Second Grade	Third Grade
KEY IDEAS AND DETAILS			
With prompting and support, retell familiar stories, including key details.	Retell stories, including key details, and demonstrate understanding of their central message or lesson.	Ask and answer who, what, where, when, why, and how questions to demonstrate understanding of a text.	Describe characters in a story, and explain how their actions contribute to the sequence of events.
With prompting and support, identify characters, settings, and major events in a story.	Describe characters, settings, and major events in a story, using key details.	Describe how characters in a story respond to major events and challenges.	
CRAFT AND STRUCTURE			
Recognize common types of text. Explain major differences between books that tell stories and books that give information, drawing on a wide range of text types.	Describe the overall structure of a story, including how the beginning introduces the story and how the ending concludes the action. Identify who is telling the story at various points in a text.	Acknowledge differences in the points of view of characters, including speaking in a different voice for each character when reading dialogue aloud.	

Speaking and Listening Standards

Kindergarten	First Grade	Second Grade	Third Grade
PRESENTATION OF KNOWLEDGE AND IDEAS			
Describe familiar people, places, things, and events, and with prompting and support, provide additional detail.	Describe people, places, things, and events with relevant details, expressing ideas and feelings clearly.	Tell a story or recount an experience with appropriate facts and relevant, descriptive details, speaking audibly in coherent sentences.	Tell a story or recount an experience with appropriate facts and relevant, descriptive details, speaking audibly in coherent sentences.
Add drawings or other visual displays to descriptions as desired to provide additional detail.	Add drawings or other visual displays to descriptions when appropriate to clarify ideas, thoughts, and feelings.	Create audio recordings of stories or poems; add drawings or other visual displays to stories or recounts of experiences, when appropriate, to clarify ideas, thoughts, and feelings.	Create audio recordings of stories or poems; add drawings or other visual displays to stories or recounts of experiences, when appropriate, to clarify ideas, thoughts, and feelings.

Using Oral Mentor Texts to Teach Writing

O ur early work with telling oral class stories focused on developing
vocabulary and language structure. While we were pleased that this strategy was successful, we noticed that the targeted skills we built into the
story also began showing up in our students' independent writing. The
transfer happened naturally and almost immediately. We now use the oral class story
explicitly as a major tool in our writing instruction.

Oral Class Stories Help Writers Find and Write Stories

Finding the stories of their lives can be a daunting task for young writers. Our experience—as both teachers of writing and teachers who write—is that getting started is
often the hardest part. Oral class stories are ongoing models of how to find stories in
every corner of one's life. Reminding students of where stories come from flows naturally when we use our own stories and those of the class to model how a story is built
and then retold.

This was Sherra's focus as she and her students composed one of their first class
stories, "The Recycling Bin Spider," about the time the class made a trip to the recycling bin and spotted a big, brown spider inside the lid. Being able to build a story
and tell it in an order that makes sense requires continuous practice. The beginning
stages of the writing process are sometimes glossed over, the assumption being that

children know the elements of story. However, these elements must be taught explicitly if students are to become successful writers.

The day after this exciting event took place, Sherra told her students that she had gone home and told the big, brown spider story to her family. She explained that in order to share the story she replayed it in her head like a movie (*visualization*), to be sure she told it in the order that things happened and didn't leave out any details. She thought through the visualization aloud so they understood exactly what she meant by "making a movie in her head." Then she shared the story, which she had recomposed to include ideas that were relevant to her students' writing work:

The Recycling Bin Spider

The other day, Mrs. Jones took our whole class out to the recycling bin to show us where to throw recycled paper.

We all gathered around the big, blue bin. Ian lifted the lid.

Tyrik screamed, "Mrs. Jones, look at that big, brown spider!"

Mrs. Jones quickly dumped the paper into the recycling bin.

"Now close that lid and leave the spider alone," ordered Mrs. Jones.

Cortland suggested that we might be able to find out what kind of spider it was by looking in a book.

The whole class was glad that the spider was not inside our classroom.

The beauty of this scenario is that every student experiences a story being born, a process that will support each of them every day in writing workshop when they are asked to find an incident in their life and recreate the sequence of events as a story. Students see that stories can be found anywhere. They have a model for how to retell a story. The class story is a solid introduction.

As the year progresses, the class identifies more and more shared experiences, turns them into class stories, and practices telling them until they achieve a polished delivery. Simultaneously, the students work their way through various units of study in writing workshop. They compose a piece of writing in each unit after first composing an oral class story. They are reminded how a story sounds when it is told orally and taught that it should sound the same when it is written down.

A huge benefit of the oral class story is that students develop a knack for spotting the small-moment stories of their lives. When a child catches a ladybug on the playground we hear, "Mrs. Dierking, this could be a story!" When the fire alarm sounds during reading workshop we hear, "Mrs. Jones, this could be a story." Generating story ideas is no longer a problem.

Class stories also generate connections. If we tell the class story about catching a lizard behind the bookshelf and setting him free outside, several students tell their own "lizard catching" stories. If we tell the class story about the time Joshua lost his tooth during lunch, we have a room full of students eager to tell their own stories about losing a tooth. If we build a class story about spiders that includes how a spider builds a web, students flock to the spider-book tub in the classroom library to learn more about spiders. If we include a persuasive letter in a story about the messy class-room, persuasive letters become popular at the writing center.

Telling stories is contagious; the more students do it, the better they get at it. And the better they get at it, the more they want to do it. The payoff? Good storytellers become good story writers.

Oral Class Stories Support Whole-Group Writing Instruction

Once we have found a topic for an oral story, built the story to include the craft we want to pre-teach and/or reinforce, and practiced telling the story, it becomes a very important tool for teaching writing. We shine a spotlight on each skill and strategy highlighted in the class story, and students transfer these same skills and strategies into their own stories.

Suppose we have built, practiced, and performed several class stories that collec-tively contain a sound lead, a weather lead, dialogue, varied sentence structures, and strong verbs. We now want to teach our students to revise their individual stories by rewriting their lead and using strong verbs. We remind students of the class sto-ries' beginnings, how we chose a sound lead for one and a weather lead for another because always using the same type of lead would be boring. We revise for stronger verbs, reminding students of the role strong verbs have played in specific class stories.

Writing minilessons is often linked to an effective skill introduced in a class story. For example, here is an example of how we connect a class story to how writers should use strong verbs:

Writers, yesterday I was hurrying to get ready for school so I had to get dressed really fast. Right before I walked out the door, I glanced in the mirror, grabbed my purse, and headed out to my car. All of a sudden, in the back of my mind,

I thought, *Hmm. Something didn't look right*. So I went back to the mirror to take a second look. The something that didn't look right was my slippers! I was in such a hurry I forgot to put on my shoes! I am so glad that I went back to take that second look.

Today I want to teach you how writers go back and take a second look by checking for wimpy verbs. Think back to our "Year of the Duck" class story. Let's remember it together by saying it out loud:

> It is hard to believe that we are in third grade. Some friends we already know, but some friends are new. We were just settling in to get to know each other when the loudest noise we had ever heard came across the intercom. It sounded like a wounded duck. "What is going on?" inquired Mrs. Dierking. Everyone was holding their hands over their ears. The sound, *akkk-akkk-akkk*, wouldn't stop. Mrs. Dierking flung open the door to ask Mrs. Stewart if she knew what was happening. Mrs. Stewart's students were acting just like we were! Their hands were over their ears and their mouths were shaped in a big round *O*. Both teachers huddled in the hallway discussing the matter. Finally, just as we were about to leave our room and possibly the building to get away from that atrocious noise, it stopped. What an interesting way to start third grade. We are going to call it "The Year of the Duck."

When I built this story I wanted our listeners to picture how I threw the door open really hard, so I chose the word *flung*. I used the word *huddled* to show how Mrs. Stewart and I were standing close together, talking. These are picture-painting action words called verbs. All verbs are not created equal. Some verbs do a better job at showing the reader action. These are called strong verbs. *Flung* and *huddled* are strong verbs. We used strong verbs in our class story, and now I want you to use them as you revise your own stories.

Go back to your written pieces today and take a second look. Just as we retold our class story, I want you to reread your piece. Be on the lookout for places you can change your verbs to make them stronger. Paint a picture for your reader like we painted in our oral story.

The craft modeled in a class story can be brought out again and again to show how the same strategy is effective in a written story. For more examples of minilessons that use the class story and a list of potential teaching points see Oral Class Stories in Whole-Class Writing Lessons on page 84.

Oral Class Stories Support One-to-One Writing Instruction

We also use oral class stories—which students know inside out—as we help them make decisions about their writing in one-to-one conferences. Every student is able to call on these texts at any moment without needing to have them physically in hand. We can refer to them and be certain they will know what we are highlighting: "Remember how we did this work in the class story? Now try it out in your written story."

Connie thinks this aspect of the oral story is the "bee's knees." She was constantly misplacing her mentor texts. She'd be in the middle of a great conference, ready to show the perfect example, when, low and behold, it wasn't in her conferring folder. Carrying the oral mentor text in her head and knowing it also lives in the heads of her students makes her conferring stronger.

For example, during a recent fall writing workshop, Connie sat beside Lydia for a conference. Lydia's story about riding in her dad's truck when it got a flat tire began, "My dad's truck had a flat tire." Connie reminded Lydia of a class story that began with a sound lead. Lydia immediately repeated the first sentence: *Boom! Boom! The thunder shook the windows of our classroom like a wind chime.* Remembering that this sentence had been the favorite of several people who had listened to the story, Lydia decided to try a sound lead in her own story. Her new first sentence: *Pop! Bang! Bump! The tire went flat.*

When we practice a class story, we showcase the purposeful decisions we've made as a storyteller. The bigger deal we make of each craft technique, the greater chance our students will try it out in their own writing. Like any other coach, we are saying, "Watch how I do this work. We can practice together until you are ready to try it on your own." We constantly encourage our students to try these techniques in their independent writing and to be on the lookout for other authors who use the techniques. Once a class story is polished and celebrated, we can dip back into it at any time, using it as a mentor text as we make or review a teaching point.

We are astonished by how easily our students are able to transfer the writer's craft highlighted in our class stories to their own writing. They feel free to try something in print that they have already mastered "in the air." Simply reminding students of the craft modeled in the class story prompts them to use the same techniques in their own stories to bump up the writing.

Oral Class Stories Teach Writing Craft

We want our students to muck around with words and phrases, always looking for opportunities to improve their drafts. Students are drawn to writing craft with which they feel comfortable. The writing techniques we highlight in oral class stories (mentioned in Chapter 2)—moves we strive to transfer into students' independent writing—follow.

Craft Techniques Highlighted in Oral Class Stories

- » Strong leads
- » Strong endings
- » Dialogue
- » Story language
- » Speaker tags
- » Adjectives
- » Varied sentence structures
- » Precise verbs
- » English grammar and usage
- » Rich vocabulary
- » Elaboration
- » Similes
- » Alliteration
- » Repeating lines
- » Temporal words
- » Onomatopoeia
- » Magic three
- » Slowing down a moment
- » Ellipses
- » Inserting a poem or song
- » Inserting a fact
- » Inserting a how-to box
- » Inserting a letter

Strong Leads

Every story needs a strong beginning. Young children tend to stick with one kind of lead. Many of our students start every story with, *One day*. Others like starting a story with a question: *Do you have a pet? Have you ever lost a tooth? Do you like pizza?* To help our students realize that stories can start in many ways, we intentionally start each class story with a different lead. For example:

> » Weather: *Late one stormy summer afternoon . . .*
> » Question: *How many times have you caught a lizard?*
> » Sound: *Drip, drop, drip, drop! It started raining right before recess.*
> » Quotation: *"Pick me up at noon," I shouted to my mom.*
> » Feeling: *It was the scariest storm of the year.*
> » Hint: *You'll never believe what happened the day we went on a listening walk.*

Whatever lead we choose, we name it and point out that we are starting the class story this way on purpose. We tell our students that the super fun thing about being writers is that we get to be the boss of the words, that we are choosing to start this class story with a particular kind of lead. Because we vary leads from story to story, our young writers hear how effective particular leads can be and are able to make an informed choice when deciding which lead works best for their story (see Figures 4.1 and 4.2).

Our students maintain a mental checklist of leads, and we encourage metacognition: "Oh yeah, I remember in the snake story we used a weather lead to show our listeners how hot the sidewalk was where the snake was laying. I want my reader to know that I was freezing while I waited in line at the football game, so I could start my story with a weather lead." Trying on class story leads as possibilities for their own stories allows our students to be the boss!

Strong Endings

Many young writers believe they can wrap up a story with the words *The End*. But they just stop writing, leaving the reader feeling the story isn't over. Ending a story requires the ability to summarize, a high-level skill for developing writers. Just as we vary the way we begin each class story, we vary how we end each story. For example:

> » Circular: *Starting and ending the story with the same sentence.*
> » Feeling: *We wondered with sadness if we would ever see the butterflies again.*
> » Question: *Would you like to go to the playground again next week?*

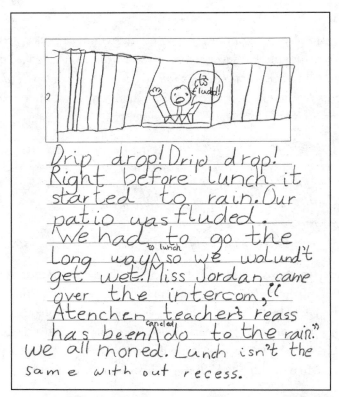

Drip, drop! Drip, drop! Right before lunch it started to rain. Our patio was flooded. We had to go the long way to lunch so we wouldn't get wet. Miss Jordan came over the intercom, "Attention teachers, recess has been canceled due to the rain." We all moaned. Lunch isn't the same without recess.

Figure 4.1 Joshua includes a sound lead in his individual story.

» Twist: *Poppy left our classroom with a big smile on his face. Little did we know what he had in store for his next visit.*

Again, whatever ending we use, we name it and tell our students we chose it for a reason. Then, as we do with leads, we encourage students to think back to every ending of every class story (symbol grids help them remember) and decide which one sounds best for their own piece. We ask them to remember the feeling of wrapping up the story and to consider the words used to create this feeling (see Figure 4.3). We often display an anchor chart of the types of endings used in class stories, as suggestions for students to try.

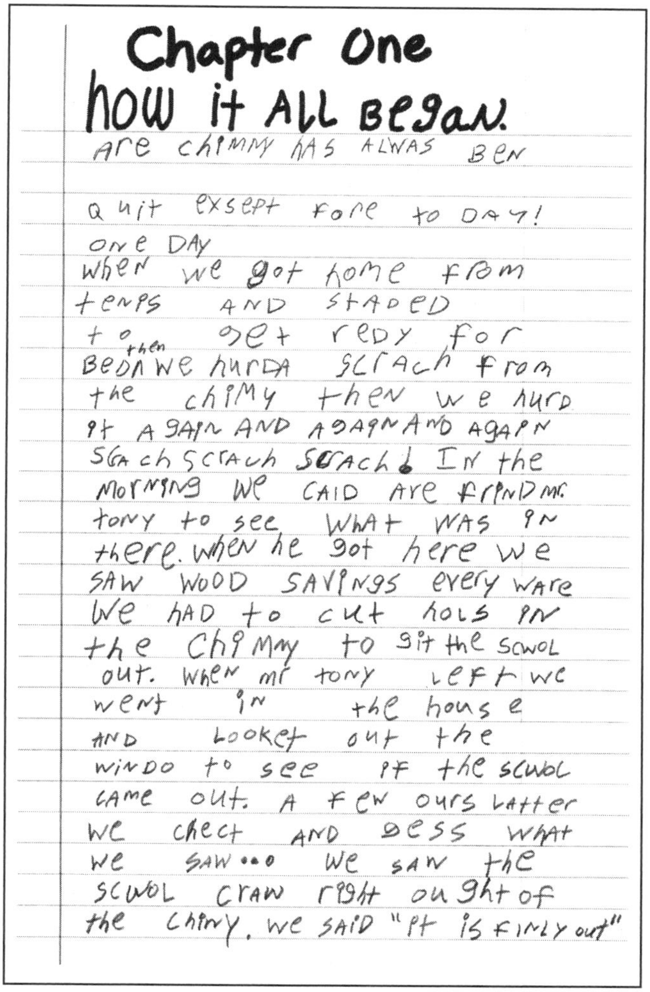

> # Chapter One
> ## how it ALL BEgan.
> Are chimny has Alwas Ben
> quit exsept fore to Day!
> one DAy
> when we got home from
> tenps and staDED
> to then set reDy for
> Beon we hurDA scrach from
> the chimy then we hurd
> it a gain and agaqn and agapn
> scach scrach scrach in the
> morning we caid Are frpnd mr.
> tony to see what was in
> there. when he got here we
> saw wood savings every ware
> we had to cut hols pn
> the chimny to git the scwol
> out. when mr tony left we
> went in the house
> and looket out the
> windo to see pf the scwol
> came out. A few ours latter
> we chect and Dess what
> we saw ... we saw the
> scwol craw right ought of
> the chimny. we said "pt is finly out"

Our chimney has always been quiet except for today. One day, when I got home from tennis and started to get ready for bed, we heard a scratch from the chimney. Then we heard it again and again and again. Scratch, scratch, scratch! In the morning, we called our friend, Mr. Tony, to see what was in there. When he got here, we saw wood shavings everywhere. We had to cut holes in the chimney to get the squirrel out. When Mr. Tony left, we went in the house and looked out the window to see if the squirrel came out. A few hours later, we checked and guess what we saw . . . we saw the squirrel crawl right out of the chimney. We said, "It is finally out."

Figure 4.2 Anthony uses a hint lead mirroring a lead from a class story.

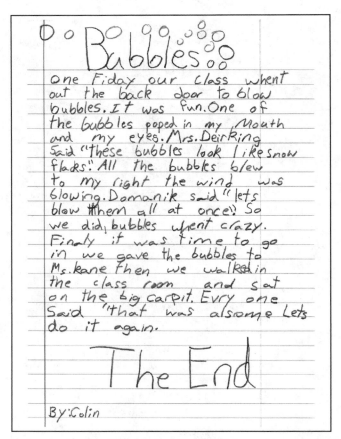

One Friday, our class went outside to blow bubbles. It was fun. One of the bubbles popped in my mouth and my eyes. Mrs. Dierking said, "Those bubbles look like snowflakes." All the bubbles blew to my right. The wind was blowing. Dominick said, "Let's blow them all at once." So we did. The bubbles went crazy. Finally, it was time to go in. We gave the bubbles to Mrs. Kane. Then we walked in the classroom and sat on the big carpet. Everyone said, "That was awesome; let's do it again."

Figure 4.3 Colin tries out a feeling ending.

Dialogue

Dialogue makes any story more interesting. When a storyteller or writer makes a character speak, the listener or reader has a better sense of who that character is. The Common Core standards state that students need to be able to recount an event or short sequence of events using details, including the characters' actions, feelings, and thoughts. An effective way to get this information across is to include dialogue. Since class stories center on shared class experiences, it's easy to use dialogue in every story, probably more than once. We remind our students that sentences with dialogue are the ones they love to retell and help them understand that is because dialogue brings a story to life. We have them find places in their own stories that will be enhanced by dialogue. Putting words in the mouths of characters is empowering. Students love hearing their own voices in a story. Dialogue shows up in our students' writing immediately (see Figure 4.4).

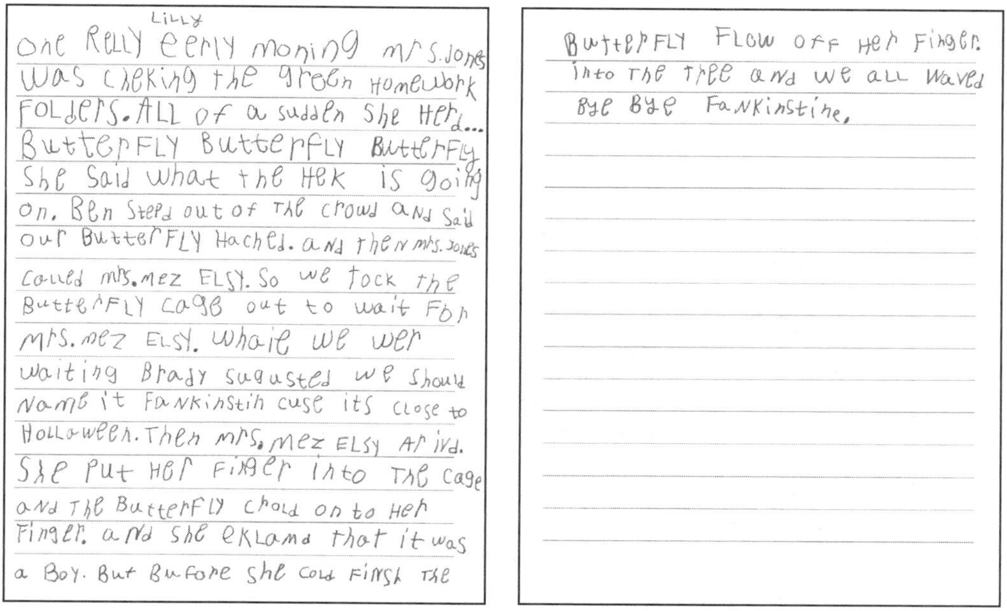

Lilly
One Relly eerly moning mrs.Jones
was cheking the green Homework
Folders. All of a sudden she Herd...
Butterfly butterfly butterfly
She said what the Hek is going
on. Ben steped out of the crowd and said
our butterfly haced. and then mrs. Jones
coued mrs.mez Elsy. So we tock the
butterfly cage out to wait Fon
mrs.mez Elsy. whaie we wer
waiting Brady sugusted we should
name it Fankinstin cuse its close to
Holloween. Then mrs.mez Elsy arivd.
She put her finger into the cage
and the butterfly choud on to her
finger. and she eklamd that it was
a boy. But bufore she cold finsh the

butterfly flow off her finger
into the tree and we all waved
bye bye Fankinstine,

One really early morning, Mrs. Jones was checking the green homework folders. All of a sudden, she heard, "Butterfly, butterfly, butterfly." She said, "What the heck is going on?" Ben stepped out of the crowd and said, "Our butterfly hatched." And then Mrs. Jones called Mrs. Metz-Easely. So we took the butterfly cage out to wait for Mrs. Metz-Easely. While we were waiting, Brady suggested, "We should name it Frankenstein because it's close to Halloween. Then Mrs. Metz-Easely arrived. She put her finger into the cage and the butterfly crawled onto her finger. She exclaimed that it was a boy. But before she could finish, the butterfly flew off her finger into the tree. We all waved, bye-bye Frankenstein.

Figure 4.4 Lilly attempts to make people talk in her story.

Story Language

Using story language requires knowing how stories go. Since we want our class stories to sound like a book, we mirror the formal language used in written texts. For example:

» *On the other hand*
» *Out of the corner of my eye*
» *All of a sudden*
» *Out of the blue*
» *A long time ago*
» *As a matter of fact*
» *Before too long*

Keeping a running chart of the story language we use and challenging students to include it in their own stories helps them transfer this strategy to their writing and become "story language detectives" in their reading (see Figures 4.5 and 4.6).

Figure 4.5 Story Language Anchor Chart Used for Class Story and Individual Writing Pieces

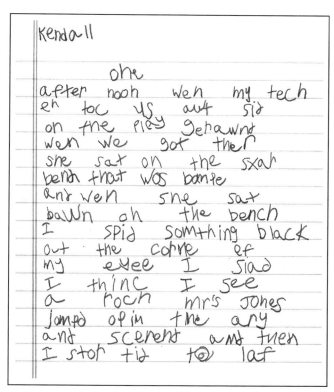

Kendall

one
after noon wen my tech
en toc us aut sid
on the play gehawnd
wen we got ther
she sat on the sxar
benh that was bonpe
ant wen she sat
baWn on the bench
I spid somthing black
out the conre ef
my eyee I siad
I thinc I see
a roch mr's jones
jomod ofin the any
ant scerent ant then
I stop tid to laf

One afternoon my teacher took us outside to the playground. When we got there she sat on the square bench that was bumpy and when she sat down on the bench I spied something black out the corner of my eye. I said, "I think I see a roach." Mrs. Jones jumped up in the air and screamed and then I started to laugh.

Figure 4.6 Kendall uses story language.

Speaker Tags

Speaker tags allow listeners and readers to envision how a character is saying something. In every class story we make a big deal about using better words than the wimpy *said*, which doesn't allow listeners or readers to paint a picture in their head. (Examples include *exclaimed, shouted, scolded, inquired, cried, whispered, giggled,* and *hollered.*) Retelling an oral class story shows our students that explaining how the character says something improves the story. During a retelling, students change their voices to match the speaker tag.

Adjectives

Adjectives describe people, places, or things, giving more meaning to these nouns. The Common Core standards require that kindergartners understand frequently used adjectives. Adjectives strengthen the oral class story, and omitting them from a retelling reveals the drab result. We ask our students to reread their stories as "description detectives" and decide whether they are gray or colorful. We also have students retell a class story and add punch to every adjective used, then do the same with their own stories. If little punching goes on, our writers know they need to return to their pieces and add some description.

We deliberately teach children words categorized as adjectives and include them in our class stories. One year Connie's students scoured their oral class stories and found words describing the taste of ice cream, the color of a puppy's fur, and how a seashell felt to the touch. They recorded each adjective on a sticky note and posted the sticky notes on an anchor chart under the appropriate headings: *Words That Describe Taste*, *Words That Describe Sound*, *Words That Describe Emotion*, and so on. Every time they used a new adjective in a new class story, they added a new sticky note to the chart. The words on the chart soon began to appear in their written stories, because they now understand their purpose (see Figure 4.7).

Varied Sentence Structures

Variety is the spice of life. Interesting stories contain varied sentences. Some sentences are short; others are long. Some sentences are connected with a conjunction; others are not. Some repeat important statements; others tell the reader what is important in short word bursts. Stories that keep us reading use varied sentences. According to the Common Core standards, students need to be able to *produce, expand, and complete simple and compound declarative, interrogative, imperative, and exclamatory sentences in response to prompts*.

We teach this writing technique by pointing out and categorizing varied sentences. Suppose the following sentences are in a class story: *Mrs. Jones was having a bad day. She was late for school and she couldn't find her glasses*. We point out that the second sentence is really two sentences joined with the word *and*. Or, we have students identify the nouns and verbs in the class story sentences and notice whether the nouns precede or follow the verbs.

Retelling the story, students see that varied class story sentences encourage reader engagement. We remind them that none of our listeners ever said, "Your story was

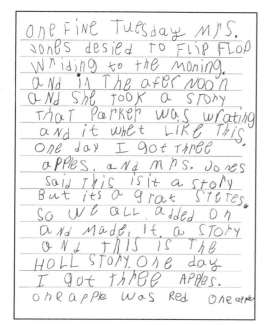 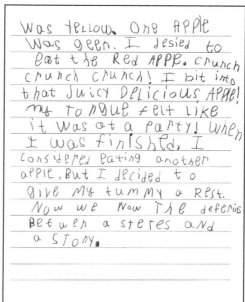

One fine Tuesday, Mrs. Jones decided to flip flop, writing in the morning instead of the afternoon. She took a story that Parker was writing and it went like this: One day I got three apples. And Mrs. Jones said, "This isn't a story, but it's a great sentence." So we all added on and made it a story. This is the whole story: One day, I got three apples. One apple was red. One apple was yellow. One apple was green. I decide to eat the red apple. My tongue felt like it was at a party! When I was finished, I considered eating another apple, but I decided to give my tummy a rest. Now we know the difference between a sentence and a story.

Figure 4.7 Ava experiments with adjectives borrowed from the class story.

boring. Every sentence started the same." The class story sentences are different lengths, different structures, different types (see Figure 4.8).

Then we encourage students to examine their writing for different types of sentences. If they underline the nouns in their stories in one color and the verbs in another, they quickly see whether they have used only one type of sentence. Underlining conjunctions lets them identify their compound sentences. During conferences we use class story sentences to help our young writers vary their sentences' structure and length.

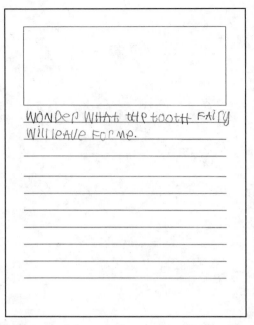

ONe NiGHt i WAS eAtiNG
My DiNNer yum yum yum
i Felt SomethiNG WPONG
there WAS SOMethiNG HAPD.
i PUlleD it Out ANo it WAS My
tooth i WAS thrilleD i GAve
it to My DAD FOP SAFe KePPiNG AS
SOON AS i Got HOMe. i BeGGeD My
DAD to Give it to Me AS SOON AS i HAo it
i DASHeD to My POOM AS QUiCK AS A
WiNK i PUt it UNDer My Pillow. i

WONDer WHAt the tooth FAiry
WillleAve FOP Me.

One night I was eating my dinner. Yum! Yum! Yum! I felt something wrong. There was something hard. I pulled it out and it was my tooth. I was thrilled. I gave it to my dad for safe keeping. As soon as I got home, I begged my dad to give it to me. As soon as I had it, I dashed to my room as quick as a wink. I put it under my pillow. I wonder what the tooth fairy will leave for me.

Figure 4.8 Andrew uses many types of sentences as modeled through the class story.

Precise Verbs

Georgia Heard, in *Awakening the Heart*, says, "Verbs are the engines of sentences, and the more abstract they are the less powerful the engine" (1991, 83). The class story lets students practice hearing and identifying the verbs in sentences. Taking a verb in a class story and identifying a range of more and less precise related meanings shows students that verb precision clarifies and deepens a story's meaning (see Figure 4.9). Paint chips are a great graphic organizer for this: We write the verb from the mentor class story on the middle paint chip. Then, with our students' help, we write less precise verbs on the paint chips above and more precise verbs on the paint chips

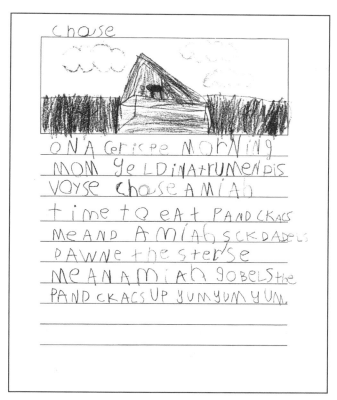

One crisp morning, mom yelled in a tremendous voice, "Chase! Amiah! Time to eat pancakes." Me and Amiah skedaddled down the stairs. Me and Amiah gobbled the pancakes up. Yum! Yum! Yum!

Figure 4.9 Chase includes strong verbs.

below. This exercise helps students get a sense of the continuum of verb precision so that they are more able to identify and use precise verbs in their own stories.

We always encourage young writers to use verbs that convey the action in the story accurately. Moving students away from the overtired *went* is not as easy as it seems, but our students are now used to us pointing out better alternatives. Near the end of every year we retell a class story replacing our action verbs with *went*. Inevitably the students shout, "No! You've made our story boring!" Then they retell the story as it should sound, with precise verbs.

English Grammar and Usage

The Common Core standards, at every grade level, stress a command of standard English grammar and usage when writing or speaking. The class story is the perfect venue for modeling how to use proper nouns, possessive nouns, pronouns, and prepositions. After introducing these types of words in the class story, we state that the story "sounds right" because it uses proper English grammar and usage. (Retelling the story using incorrect grammar lets students hear the difference.) Then we encourage our students to transfer this knowledge to their writing. We remind them how the class story sounded and ask them to compare their grammar with that of their class story. "Remember the first line of our possum story? Say it with me. 'Mrs. Dierking, come quick, there is a possum in the tree.' That sentence makes sense, right? Now read your first sentence. Does that sentence sound right to you? What is missing?"

Rich Vocabulary

We introduce new vocabulary in every class story. A rich vocabulary is an essential aspect of literacy, and class stories lend themselves to teaching new words both implicitly and explicitly. This strong vocabulary easily spills over into students' individual writing.

It has been said that the printed word is silent and still because there are no environmental clues. Students out in nature understand the difference between *dusk* and *dawn* because the sky looks different. However, when they read these words in the classroom, there are no visual clues—all they see are the words. Including as yet unknown words in the context of a class story helps our students live these words.

One day Connie was reading to her students gathered on the rug. Suddenly they heard a lot of noise coming from the vestibule they shared with another classroom. Connie stopped reading and asked, "What is all that ruckus coming from the vestibule?" Without being told a formal definition, students knew *ruckus* was a word standing for a lot of noise and *vestibule* was a name for the shared space between the classrooms. They knew because it was a direct experience. They were there, they lived it. When Connie turned that shared experience into a class story, she made sure she included this sentence, because she wanted her students to be able to use those words in conversation or in their writing.

The best part of teaching vocabulary words to young writers is they aren't afraid to try them out. Although we want to keep the oral story oral, we post a list of new words used in every class story. Students are eager to find places in their own stories to try out these new words.

Elaboration

We encourage our young writers to "tell more about the sentence before." Teaching and practicing elaboration takes time. Adding the word *really* twenty times is not elaboration. Elaboration is including the tiny actions, the dialogue, the sights and sounds and feelings of the character. It can be easily modeled in an oral class story. Because we deliberately build these stories to include what we want to model, we can pull out one of them and name the sentences that elaborate a big idea. The following description of a class story's main character, a lizard, is one type of elaboration:

> "Mrs. Dierking, there's a lizard in the boys bathroom!" cried Evan. Mrs. Dierking hurried into the vestibule. *[tell me more]* The lizard was perched on the edge of the sink. *[tell me more]* It appeared to be a baby lizard. *[tell me more]* He was light brown and about the size of a grown-up's finger.
>
> Evan yelled, "I can catch it!" *[tell me more]* He attempted to catch the creature with his bare hand, but the lizard was too quick. *[tell me more]* It darted under the sink and out of sight. "Oh well," sighed Mrs. Dierking. "We'll have to keep our eye out for our new class pet!"

The three sentences telling more about the lizard in the bathroom and the two sentences telling more about Evan's trying to catch the lizard help provide elaboration so that listeners/readers can better visualize the story.

The next step is for students to include elaboration in their own stories. Once our writers have completed a first draft, we ask them to use three different-colored pencils to underline their elaboration sentences. If they can't find any sentences that tell more about a character, it's time for a conference. We want students to know that a story without elaboration can make sense but it won't be very interesting. Elaboration always draws in the audience and makes a story sound better (see Figure 4.10).

Similes/Metaphors

Young writers love to experiment with similes and metaphors. Pointing out a simile or metaphor in an oral mentor text during a lesson always brings an acknowledging nod. Suppose the teaching point for writing workshop is to teach students how to paint a picture using a simile. How lovely to dip back into a story the students know by heart and point out evidence of this writer's trick. Students pick out the symbol that represents the simile, and then the games begin. They rewrite the simile so that it still makes sense. Or, we rewrite the simile once so that it makes sense and again so that

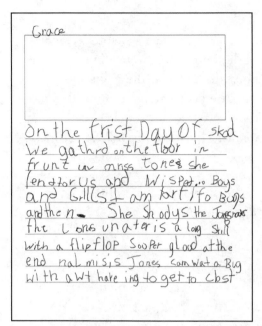
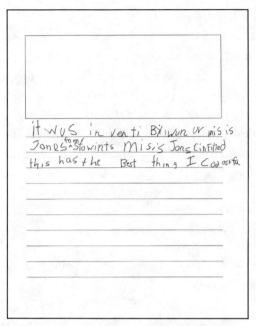

Grace

on the frist Day of skool
we gathrd on the floor in
frunt uv mnss tones she
lendtor us and Wispet... Boys
and Grlls I am trf/fo Bugs
and then. She sh.odys the Jongsnator
the L ons un ater is a long still
with a flipflop Sooper glood at the
end nal misis Jones somwat a Bug
with a Wt hake ing to get to cbst

it wus in venti Bx iwun ur mis is
Jones Stowints misi's Jons CinFitied
this has the Best thing I caaosrta

On the first day of school, we gathered on the floor in front of Mrs. Jones. She leaned toward us and whispered, "Boys and girls, I am terrified of bugs!" And then . . . she showed us the Jones-a-nator. The Jones-a-nator is a long stick with a flip-flop super glued to the end. Now Mrs. Jones can swat a bug without having to get too close. It was invented by one of Mrs. Jones's former students. Mrs. Jones confided, "This is the best thing I could ever have."

Figure 4.10 Grace elaborates, telling more about the Jones-a-nator.

it does not, and then students are invited to have a conversation with a partner about why one works and the other doesn't.

One of Connie's class stories contained the sentence, *We stood as quiet as a mouse waiting for the snake to move.* Her students thought of many other similes that would have worked in the class story:

» *Our bodies were as stiff as a board.*
» *We stood as quiet as a sleeping baby.*
» *We stopped like a train on the track.*

When Connie offered, "We stood as quiet as a rock waiting for the snake to move," several students raised their eyebrows, confused. They didn't like this new suggestion. They decided that a rock isn't really quiet, it's just a thing that lies there. The rock simile didn't paint the appropriate picture.

These kinds of discussions help students make good choices in the craft they incorporate into their writing. Students usually don't struggle to create similes or metaphors, but they do struggle to create ones that make sense. The class story models how similes and metaphors should help readers envision the story, not be used just because they are fun to write.

Alliteration

Children also love to play around with alliteration. Beginning as many words in a sentence with the same sound is a great exercise in phonemic awareness and creates some very interesting sentences. As soon as this technique is introduced in a class story, our students give it a go in their own writing. Using alliteration purposely in a class story takes planning, however.

One of Sherra's favorite class stories is "Pumpkin Project Day"; the final line is *Pumpkin Project Day was practically perfect*. This sentence is her model for alliteration in any story. She demonstrates how much fun it is to say the line, but makes it clear that alliteration can appear in any sentence of a story (see Figure 4.11).

Repeating Lines

Repeating lines are common in the texts young writers hear read aloud. Teaching students that a repeating line signifies importance is not difficult. The tricky part is helping students determine *what* is important for readers to know about, the setting or the character or the main event. Using repeating lines in a class story allows us to scaffold how to choose an important part. It also lets students hear how a well-placed repeating line sounds. We also have them look through picture books in the classroom library for additional examples.

It takes practice before students are able to use a repeating line effectively in their own pieces. Sherra included a repeating line in "Pumpkin Project Day"—*Today is Pumpkin Project Day*—after each sentence to keep reminding listeners that the story was about a very special day. Later her writers began their own stories with a repeating line that restated the topic and identified the spot(s) in their story where repeating it made sense.

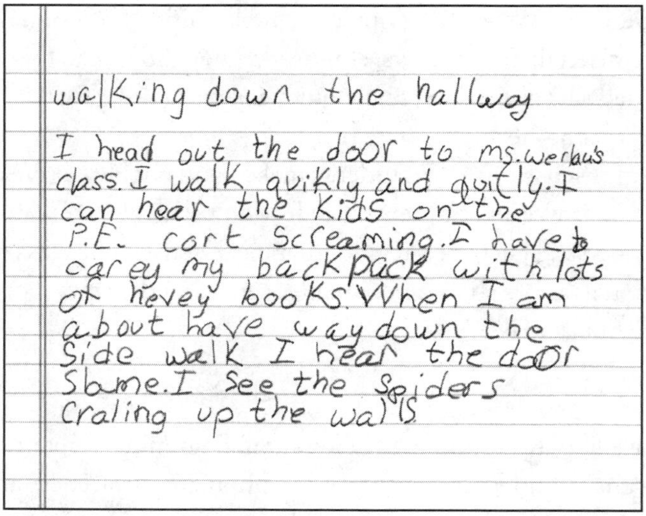

> walking down the hallway
>
> I head out the door to ms. werlau's class. I walk quikly and quitly. I can hear the kids on the P.E. cort screaming. I have to carey my backpack with lots of hevey books. When I am about have way down the side walk I hear the door Slame. I see the spiders craling up the walls

I head out the door to Ms. Werlau's class. I walk quickly and quietly. I can hear the kids on the P.E. court screaming. I have to carry my backpack with lots of heavy books. When I am about half way down the sidewalk, I hear the door slam. I see the spiders crawling up the walls.

Figure 4.11 Sierra models her beginning after a class story and tries her hand at alliteration: "quickly and quietly."

Temporal Words

Temporal words (*first, to begin with, next, after that, in the meantime, finally*) signal the order of events. The ability to use these words appropriately is a Common Core standard beginning in first grade. We teach students that signaling event order is necessary if listeners are to understand the meaning of our oral class stories.

We demonstrate this importance in our writing instruction as well. One simple activity is taking a story we've written that doesn't include temporal words and cutting it up into individual sentences. Then we throw the sentences up in the air and ask students to reassemble the story. Without any signal words, this is very difficult to do.

We also display a list of temporal words used in every class story so that students see the many choices they have for signaling the order of events. Highlighting temporal words in drafts and replacing common ones with more unusual ones is an effective revision activity. When students use temporal words deliberately we know that they understand the importance of story order (see Figure 4.12).

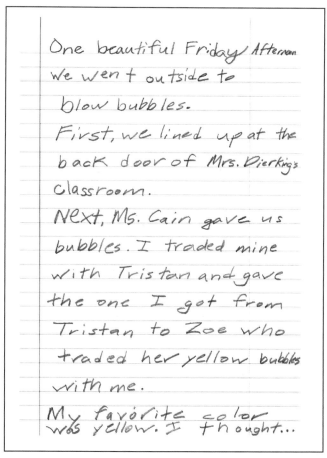

One beautiful Friday afternoon, we went outside to blow bubbles. First, we lined up at the back door of Mrs. Dierking's classroom. Next, Ms. Cain gave us bubbles. I traded mine with Tristan and gave the one I got from Tristan to Zoe who traded her yellow bubbles with me. My favorite color was yellow. I thought . . .

Figure 4.12 Hailey uses transition words on the first page of her story.

Onomatopoeia

Children love to hear sound words in stories and are delighted to learn this really cool term for them. Once we introduce sound words in class stories, they appear every-where in student writing. They are fun to use and a very effective way to bring readers into the scene. To get our students thinking about sound words we ask, "What are the sounds in our classroom? What are the sounds of night? What are the sounds of the lunchroom?"

Magic Three

Fairy tales, in particular, make great use of the power and magic of the number three. Examples, reasons, or incidents take on more weight when presented in threes. We don't incorporate this technique into every class story, but it's a strategy we want our students to be aware of.

We remind students that a series of three creates suspense and draws a scene out for the reader. Popping up a finger for each item in a set of three when retelling an oral story makes this strategy concrete. The classic fairy tales *The Three Little Pigs, The Three Bears*, and *The Three Billy Goats Gruff* are intriguing to young writers, who are eager to try the "three" technique in their own writing.

In this class story about a wind storm, Connie deliberately incorporates two sets of three:

> "Smack," the classroom door hit the side of the building like a club. "Watch out!" Mrs. Dierking announced. "The wind is awful today." As we walked out to PE *tufts of grass, leaves, and dirt* swirled around like tiny tornadoes. Our hair blew wild, and we struggled to walk against the strong wind. The dirt *stung our eyes, pelted our skin, and made us feel as if we were walking into an invisible wall.* It was so strange, where had this wind come from? Our science teacher, Mrs. Werlau, answered that question for us.

In a first-grade class story about the importance of New Year's resolutions, Sherra used three resolutions as examples, pointing out that she thought five would be too many, one just didn't seem enough, but three seemed just right. Ashley gave this technique a go when telling readers about her roller coaster ride (see Figure 4.13).

Slowing Down a Moment

Slowing down a moment in a story is a difficult concept to teach and learn. To teach the technique, we incorporate it into an oral story that has already been celebrated. First we display the symbol grid associated with the story and retell it. Then we choose one of the symbols and ask students to think back to that moment and remember everything that happened—what they saw, heard, and felt. Recently, Sherra went about it this way:

Class, remember the story about the time we all wrote New Year resolutions? Today we're going to revisit that story and use a trick called slowing down a moment. *[Points to the symbol of a pencil and paper]* This represents the sentence, *Mrs. Jones sent us off to write some New Year's resolutions of our own.* I'm going to close my eyes and think. What did that look like? What did that sound like? What did that feel like? I remember you all seemed eager to write. The team captains were quickly passing out the papers so you could get started right away. Once you started writing, it was so quiet you could hear a pin drop. As a matter of fact, the only thing I could hear was the scritch-scratching of your pencils. I can make

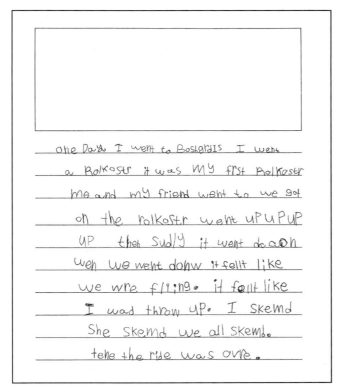

One day, I went to Busch Gardens. I went on a roller coaster. It was my first roller coaster. Me and my friend went too. We got on the roller coaster. We went up, up, up. Then suddenly, it went down. When we went down, it felt like we were flying. It felt like I would throw-up. I screamed, she screamed, we all screamed. Then the ride was over.

Figure 4.13 Note the magic three: "I screamed, she screamed, we all screamed."

the listener feel they are right there with me if I slow down that moment in writing the way I just did out loud, sharing the things that I saw and heard and thought:

> Mrs. Jones sent us off to write some New Year's resolutions of our own. We got busy right away. The team captains quickly passed out the paper. It was so quiet in the room that you could hear a pin drop. As a matter of fact, the only sound you could hear was the scritch-scratching of our pencils moving across the paper.

Do you see how I did that? I stopped at the moment I sent you off to write and I thought hard about what that moment looked like, sounded like, and felt like. Then I stuck my thoughts right there in the story to slow that moment down. Now everybody that hears our story will see and hear and feel the same things that I did. That was my goal. You can do the same thing in your own writing.

Later, in a writing workshop, we have students take one of their own stories and choose a sentence to slow down (see Figure 4.14).

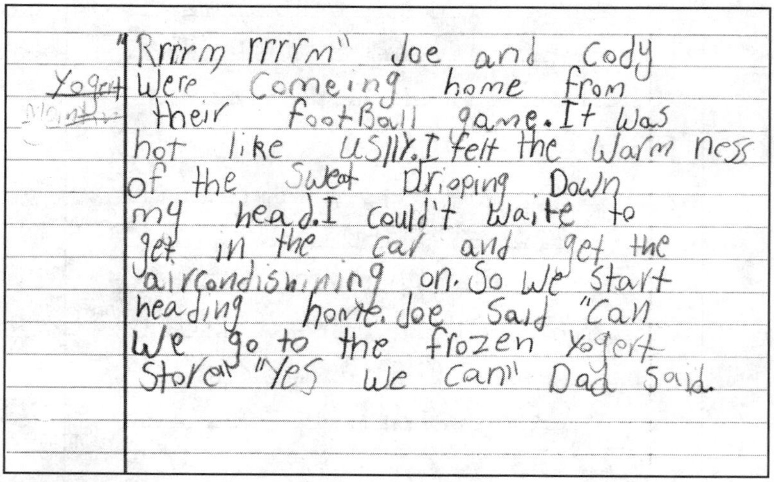
Yogert
"Rrrm rrrm" Joe and Cody
Were Comeing home from
their footBall game. It Was
hot like USllY. I felt the Warm ness
of the Sweat Driping Down
my head. I could't Waite to
get in the car and get the
aircondishining on. So We Start
heading home. Joe Said "Can
We go to the frozen Yogert
Store?" "Yes We can" Dad Said.

"Rrrm, rrrm," Joe and Cody were coming home from their football game. It was hot like usual. I felt the warmness of the sweat dripping down my head. I couldn't wait to get in the car and get the air conditioning on. So we start heading home. Joe said, "Can we go to the frozen yogurt store?" "Yes we can," said Dad.

Figure 4.14 Blake tries out the class story strategy of slowing down at the beginning.

Ellipses

Although our students are not looking at the oral class story in print, we nevertheless teach them punctuation. The ellipsis is particularly engaging. While telling the class story, we take a dramatic pause at the spot the ellipsis would appear in print. We explain that we are doing this to create suspense, to make the listener feel something is about to happen. *When we were headed back to our classroom the thunder started to roar. All of a sudden . . . CRACK! The lightning shot down from the sky.* Then, in a writing workshop we have students read one of their written stories aloud to themselves or a partner, trying out dramatic pauses. When they find an appropriate spot, we show them how to add the dot, dot, dot (see Figure 4.15).

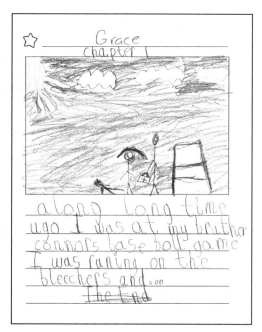
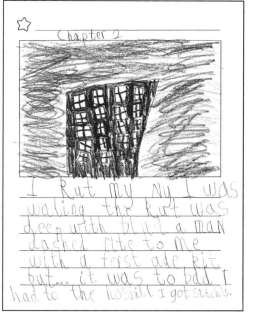

A long, long time ago, I was at my brother Conner's baseball game. I was running on the bleachers and . . . I cut my knee. I was wailing. The cut was deep with blood. A man dashed right to me with a first aid kit but . . . it was too bad. I had to go to the hospital. I got stitches.

Figure 4.15 Grace uses ellipses to create suspense.

Inserting a Poem/Song

Inserting a poem or song into an oral class story lets students see that writers can do anything they choose to make their stories fun to read. Remember Sherra's first-grade class story that included the fluency poem "Spaghetti, Spaghetti" by Jack Prelutsky? Challenging students to try the same thing in writing workshop introduced a feeling of renewed excitement

In Connie's classroom, Carly used "Twinkle, Twinkle, Little Star" as the lead to her story about camping under the stars. Trevor used the familiar "Happy Birthday" song to bring readers into his father's birthday celebration (see Figure 4.16). Highlighting the possibilities and cutting young writers loose bears amazing results.

Inserting a Fact

Providing access to both narrative and informational text is best practice in all class-rooms. A fact or two can easily be inserted into an oral class story. Connie's class story about the wind storm lent itself to inserting a few facts about the wind. A class story about a possum in the tree is a perfect opportunity to include facts about possums.

We prompt students how to do the same thing in their written narratives by asking them whether a bit of related factual information would interest their reader. A student story about the family terrier is more interesting if it includes a true fact about terriers. Terry, a writer in Connie's class, included the fact that lizards can grow up to three feet long in his story about his pet lizard (see Figure 4.17 for another example).

Inserting a How-To Box

Some class stories cry out for a how-to section or an explanation of an impor-tant object incorporated into the story. In the class story about their science expo, Connie's class included a how-to box delineating the process of conducting an exper-iment. They began the story by telling how they positioned themselves around the room in order to share their experiments. Then they interjected, "If you have never conducted a science experiment these are the steps. First, you must develop a hypoth-esis. Second, you gather your materials. . . ." Once the process had been outlined, they returned to their description of the expo. Including this hybrid structure in the class story prompted students to consider the same structure in their own writing.

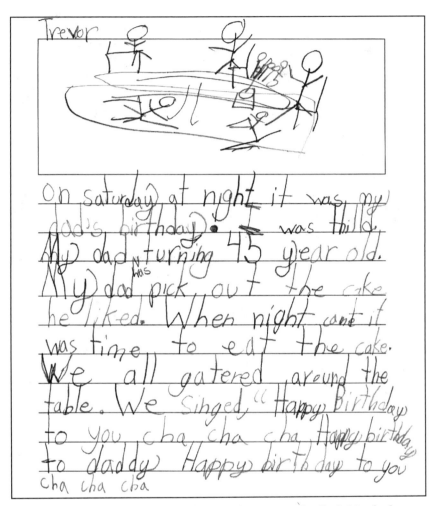

One Saturday at night, it was my dad's birthday. I was thrilled. My dad was turning 45 years old. My dad picked out the cake he liked. When night came, it was time to eat the cake. We all gathered around the table. We sang, "Happy birthday to you—cha, cha, cha—happy birthday to daddy, happy birthday to you—cha, cha, cha."

Figure 4.16

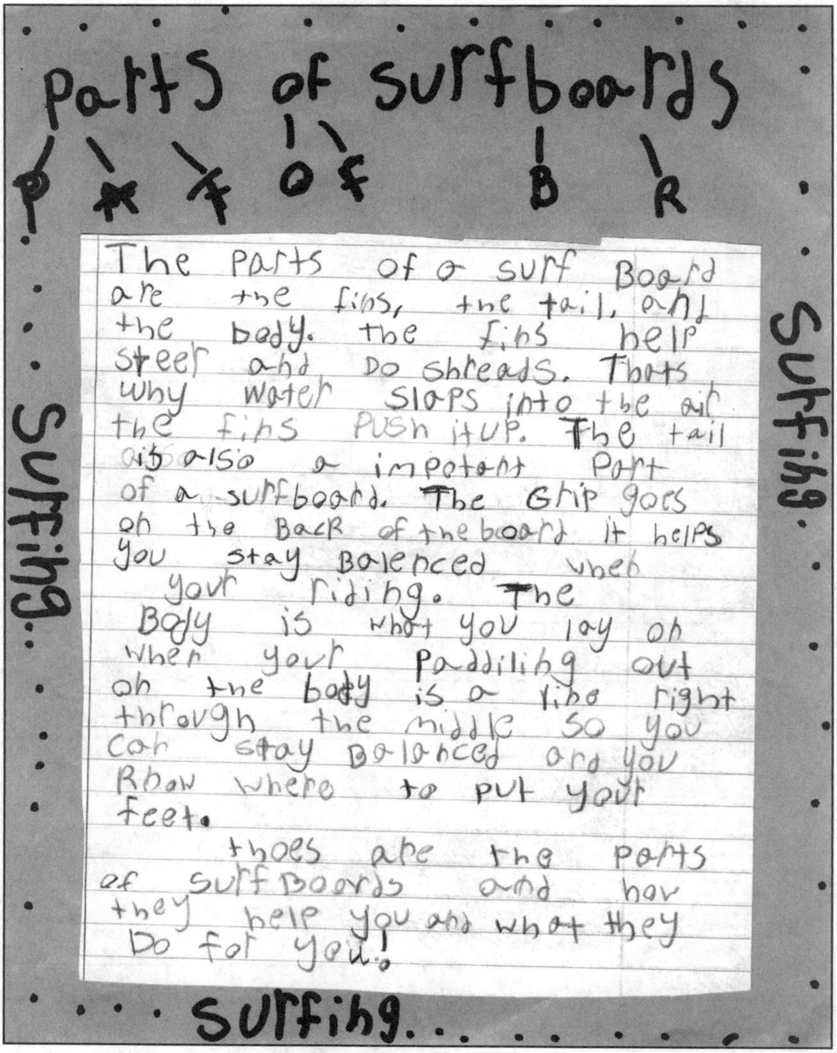

The parts of a surfboard are the fins, the tail, and the body. The fins help steer and do shreds. That's why water slaps into the air—the fins push it up. The tail is also an important part of a surfboard. The grip goes on the back of the surfboard. It helps you stay balanced when you're riding. The body is what you lay on when you're paddling out. On the body is a line right through the middle so you can stay balanced and you know where to put your feet. Those are the parts of surfboards and how they help you and what they do for you.

Figure 4.17 Gavin inserts information about surfboards inside his surfing story.

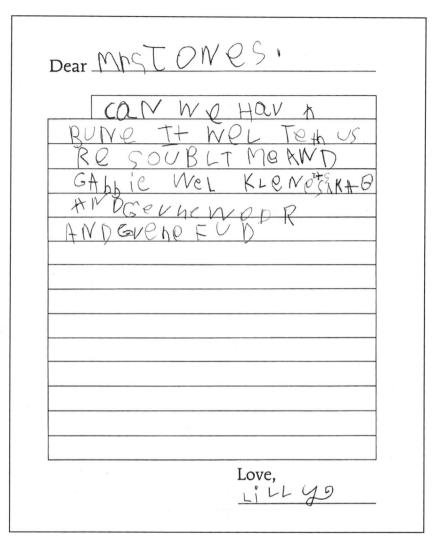

Dear _MrsTONes._

CaN We HaV a
BUNe It Wel Teh us
Re SOUBLT Me AND
GAbbie Wel KLeNe⁺ıᵏᵃᵍ
AM Geune WeⁿⁱD R
AND Guehe FUD

Love,
LiLLy

Dear Mrs. Jones,

    Can we have a bunny? It will teach us responsibility. Me and Gabbie will clean its cage and give him water and give him food.

Love,

    Lilly

Figure 4.18 Lilly's writing conference targeted how to include her letter inside a personal narrative.

Inserting a Persuasive Letter

Including a persuasive letter in a narrative may seem strange, but it's a popular device in children's literature. For example, *Click, Clack, Moo: Cows That Type*, by Dorin Cronin, is a pressing-for-change story that includes letters of persuasion throughout. Connie's class tried this technique in an oral story about how Daniel slipped on milk spilled around the lunchroom garbage can and almost hit his head. When Carly suggested they write a letter to the principal with suggestions for cleaning up the lunchroom, the persuasive letter became part of the story. This oral story was a model for students who wanted to try out this structure in their writing (see Figure 4.18).

Oral Class Stories in Whole-Class Writing Lessons

When planning for writing minilessons that make use of class stories, we discovered that most minilessons fell into these categories:

» Foundational: Lessons support foundational ideas about writing and being a writer.
» Operational: Lessons support elements of the writing process.
» Print awareness: Lessons support print awareness, conventions, and grammar.
» Craft: Lessons support writing craft moves. (Dierking and Jones, 2003)

Our minilesson work stands on the shoulders of the work done by Lucy Calkins and her colleagues at The Reading and Writing Project.

In the following section, you'll see the bare bones of a minilesson from each category, followed by a list of potential teaching points. You can also use teaching points from these minilessons when conferring with individual writers or working with small groups.

1. Writing—Foundational

Minilesson: Including a Beginning, Middle, and End

MATERIALS: MENTOR CLASS STORY WITH SYMBOLS

Connect

Tell your students that just as they have been telling class stories about events that have happened to them, they can write their own stories about things that happen to them. Both oral class stories and written stories have a beginning, middle, and end.

Teach

Display the chart paper that shows the symbols for a mentor class story. As you point to each symbol, tell the story aloud with your students. Explain that all stories have a beginning (as you point to the first few symbols), a middle (as you circle with your finger the many symbols that reflect the middle of the story), and an end (as you point to the last few symbols).

   With sticky notes, cover up the symbol or symbols that reflect the beginning.

   Tell the story aloud, leaving off the beginning, and ask students to notice how incomplete it sounds.

   Remove the sticky notes from the beginning of the story and use them to cover up the end. Tell the story aloud but don't include the ending. Comment again how the story would sound incomplete and confusing if it did not have a beginning or an ending. Finally, cover up the middle. Be sure to point out that you need many more sticky notes to cover the middle because the middle of a story is the longest part. Now tell the story leaving out the middle.

Active Engagement

Tell the students that now you will tell the story with all of the parts included. Choose a few volunteers to stand up to represent the beginning of the story. Choose a few volunteers to stand up to represent the end. The students that remain on the gathering rug can represent the middle of the story. Be sure that each group is aware of the part they are responsible for telling and then tell the story.

Link

Remind your students that when storytellers tell stories, they include a beginning, a middle, and an end, and that written stories are the same. Stories don't make sense without all three parts.

2. Writing—Operational

Minilesson: Reading Your Writing Fluently

MATERIALS: AN ORAL CLASS STORY WITH THE SYMBOLS, A TEACHER PIECE OF WRITING

Connect

With your students, tell the class story, using the symbols. When you've finished, tell students that they tell the story fluently and with expression. Just as they practiced telling the class story to make it sound that way, writers can become fluent readers of their own stories by rereading their own stories many times.

Teach

Using a piece of your own writing, read your story aloud and model struggling over some words. Model reading with determination to figure out the words that you don't know or forgot. Try to keep expression out of your voice. When you are finished with the first reading, point out that you feel proud for figuring out the tricky words, but now it is time for the practice to begin. Your goal is to read this story without struggling over any words, at an appropriate speed, and with expression in your voice. Then reread it three more times, sounding more fluent with each successive reading.

Active Engagement

Send your students to their writing folders and ask them to return to the gathering rug with a piece of their own writing. Ask them to silently reread their own story three times. When they are finished, they should share their story with a partner.

Link

Tell your students that strong writers are fluent readers of their own stories, and that they can become fluent readers of their own stories by remembering to reread their own stories many times.

3. Writing—Print Awareness

Minilesson: Writing from Top to Bottom, Left to Right

MATERIALS: A SYMBOL GRID FOR A PREVIOUS CLASS STORY, CHART PAPER/MARKER, ONE LINED SHEET OF PAPER FOR EACH STUDENT

Connect

Using an example from your life, tell your students about a time when your writing got mixed up and you were confused.

Show one of the symbol grids for an oral class story. Model telling the story from the bottom up. Ask students if it made sense.

Tell the story using the symbols from right to left. Ask students if it made sense.

Tell them that writers write stories from top to bottom and left to right, so that the story makes sense.

Teach

Using chart paper and marker, tell your students that you are going to write one of your old class stories. Remind them that you are going to write it the same way you usually tell the story using the symbols, from top to bottom and left to right. Then begin writing as you think aloud for your students. Be sure to identify that you are starting at the top left and moving to the right until you come to the end of the first line. When you are out of room, you will return all the way to the left and start again (return sweep).

Active Engagement

Give each student a sheet of lined paper. Ask them to write the first two sentences of the class story. Before they begin, have them identify where they will start their writing by pointing to the top left of the paper. Also ask them to move their finger across the first line until they come to the end. Then point to the spot they will return to when they are out of room on the first line.

Link

Remind your students that writers write the words in a story from top to bottom and left to right so that the story makes sense.

4. Writing—Craft

Minilesson: Using Proper Nouns When You Write

MATERIALS: CLASS STORY AND SYMBOL GRID

Connect

Tell your students that sometimes when you are reading the stories they have written—about the people they love, the things they like to do, and the places they like to go—you lose track of the people and places they have written about because you don't know them by name. Tell your students that you want to teach them how to make their stories easier to understand by using the real names of people and places.

Teach

Using a class story symbol grid, tell your students that you will be looking at the symbols and telling that story together. Highlight the places in the story where proper names are used, and tell students that they can do the same thing when they are writing stories. If you write the real names of people and places, the reader will feel like they know your story better.

Active Engagement

Read the following short story (or better yet, one of your own design) containing several examples of the use of proper nouns. As you read, ask your students to count each time you say the real name of a person or place. After they count, confirm their answers by showing them the story with the proper nouns highlighted.

Proper Noun Story Example:

> On the first day of summer, I had a bike race with my brother Steve. Our little sister Carrie cheered us on. We raced all the way to the end of Mulberry Street. Steve won the race, but only because our dog, Murphy, was nipping at my heels the whole way. Steve bragged the whole way back, "I'm the best bike rider in Florida!"

Link

Tell your students that as they write, they can use the real names of people and places to help readers keep track of what is happening in the story.

Sample Writing Teaching Points Using Class Stories as Mentors

FOUNDATIONAL

- Using the class story to demonstrate, teach students that writers use the details in their pictures to help remember what they want to write.
- Choose a class story and retell it as a summary, and then discuss the difference between a summary and a story. Teach your students that when writers write stories, they stay focused on one event, just as you do in the class story.

OPERATIONAL

- Use a familiar class story as a mentor for trying out something new in your own writing. (Decide beforehand what new thing you will try out, and choose your mentor class story accordingly.) Teach your students that writers can use a familiar class story as a mentor to help try new things in your own writing.
- Teach students that just as they retell an oral class story to make sure it makes sense, writers need to do the same thing. Teach them that when writers finish a writing piece, they reread the story to make sure that they have not left out any important words or details.
- Use the example of several familiar class stories as a model for how writers can find stories by paying attention to small, meaningful events in their lives.

PRINT AWARENESS

- Use familiar sentences from the class story to practice the way that writers make their stories easier to read by leaving spaces between each word.
- Demonstrate how writers spell words by saying them slowly and writing down the sounds that they hear, using familiar sentences from the oral class story. Ask students to practice on the rug with white boards before sending them off to work independently.

CRAFT

- Using a class story that uses dialogue, demonstrate how writers use quotation marks in their writing to show the reader when people are talking.

Oral Class Stories Support Conferences with Writers

Some of our students are reluctant to write. They haven't mastered the alphabetic principle, or they experience difficulty with letter/sound correspondence. Sometimes they can't come up with a topic or organize their thoughts well enough to write them down. Any number of issues can make students feel reluctant as writers. We address these issues in conferences in which we guide students through the process of creating an oral class story.

Conference 1

[This student has identified a topic for a personal story but hasn't yet attempted to write it down. When the student tells the story orally, Connie writes it down for her own reference only; the student doesn't see this written version.]

Oral Story: *Yesterday, I had a bike race with my brother. We were both pedaling really fast. I won the race.*

Compliment: You were so smart to make sure that your story had a beginning, middle, and end.

Instruction: Today I want to teach you how writers can tell more about the sentence before to make the story more interesting for the reader. We call that elaboration. Listen to my sentence: *Yesterday, I took a walk with my sister.* If I wanted to tell more about that sentence, I might say: *Yesterday, I took a walk with my sister. We decided to go around the block twice.*

Active Engagement: Now, it's your turn. Let's listen to your story. [Connie tells the story aloud and asks the student to tell more about the first sentence. After he does, she retells the story with the new sentence.] *Yesterday, I had a bike race with my brother. We raced from the end of our driveway to the stop sign at the end of our street. We were both pedaling really fast. I won the race.*

Link: That was fabulous! You told more about a sentence in your story and that made it more interesting for your reader. Remember, that's called elaborating. You did it in this story and you can do it from now on in any story you write.

The Wrap-Up: We'll work some more on this story in our next conference.

Conference 2

[During the conference Connie reminds the student how to add symbols so he can practice telling the story the same way every time.]

Compliment: The last time we conferred, you told me the story of the time you had a bike race with your brother. Then you made your story even better by elaborating. Remember how you told how you raced from the end of the driveway to the stop sign at the end of the street? Really smart work!

Instruction: So this was your story: *Yesterday, I had a bike race with my brother. We raced from the end of our driveway to the stop sign at the end of our street. We were both pedaling really fast. I won the race.* Today I want to remind you how to use symbols to help you remember how your story goes. That way you can practice your story the same way every time. Watch how I create a symbol for the first sentence of your story. [Connie orally thinks through her reasons for choosing a symbol and draws it on a piece of grid paper.]

Active Engagement: Now it's your turn to create a symbol. [The student creates a symbol for each of the remaining sentences.] Now point to your symbols and tell me your story.

Link: So now you are ready to write your story. Use your symbols to remember how each sentence goes.

[While these conferences are very brief, they get a reluctant writer or an English language learner moving forward.]

Oral Class Stories Provide Additional Practice in Writing Centers

While we insist that the class story remain oral while students are learning it and practicing it to perform for others, we know the power of turning oral stories into written ones. Once oral stories have been celebrated and are peripheral to our oral language instruction, they live on in our writing centers as inspirations for experimenting and playing with ideas. In our writing centers, we do the following:

1. Provide grid paper and markers for creating symbols
2. Include strips of paper and tape so students can revise their written stories and add new craft elements
3. Provide sticky notes
4. Display a menu of craft possibilities
5. Display former oral class story symbol grids
6. Encourage students to write what happened before or after the event that inspired a class story

7. Include drawing paper, markers, colored pencils, and crayons for illustrations
8. Provide mentor picture books
9. Provide small baskets of paint chips to use to create word continuums (the interesting names of paint colors are also educational!)
10. Provide blank booklets for creating picture books

In Conclusion

The class story is a powerful resource in a writing classroom. The celebration of the oral story is just the beginning. These stories are personal, relevant to the students in the room, and free! Showing students how to transfer their oral work to their written work pays big benefits.

Using Oral Mentor Texts to Teach Reading

We first used oral class stories to teach receptive and expressive language skills, oral fluency, and writing, but it soon became clear the stories were influencing our students' reading comprehension as well: They were articulating dialogue with more expression and rereading to improve their fluency. Whenever we referred to a skill modeled in a class story during a conference or a small-group or whole-class lesson, students would nod their head and apply it to their independent reading.

Comprehension strategies that can be taught using oral class stories students have internalized thoroughly include:

» Retelling
» Developing vocabulary
» Paying attention to punctuation
» Finding and using text-based evidence
» Visualizing
» Identifying the beginning, middle, and end
» Summarizing
» Identifying story elements
» Identifying character traits
» Inferring

We don't teach every one of these strategies in connection with every oral class story. Instead, we identify strategies we want to teach and then choose familiar class stories that offer opportunities to teach these strategies. In this chapter we use a single first-grade class story, "Poppy's Visit," to illustrate how to teach each comprehension strategy:

Poppy's Visit

On our way back from recess, Katie grabbed her grandfather's hand and dragged him toward our classroom. "Poppy, Poppy," she cried, "come see my classroom." At first, Katie's grandfather was a little reluctant because he thought he would be disrupting our class work. After a little coaxing from Mrs. Jones, he finally agreed to a visit. Mrs. Jones invited him to sit in the chair of honor, her very own rocking chair. We entertained Poppy with our class stories and then he returned the favor. He told us the story about the time he was climbing a trellis covered with lilacs and got stung in his ear by a bee. Now, whenever he smells the scent of lilac, he thinks of that bee sting. After we exchanged stories, Poppy joined us in a game of Buzz. Buzz is a math game that we play to practice counting. Katie's grandfather caught on right away. When we finished the game, Mrs. Jones sent us off to write stories of our own. Many of us read our stories to Katie's grandfather. We think Poppy really enjoyed his stay in first grade because he left with an enormous smile on his face. As a matter of fact, we think he'll be returning real soon.

Retelling

Retelling stories helps young children learn to sequence and describe events, which enhances reading comprehension. Retelling stories using pictures as a visual support gives English language learners an opportunity to develop their oral language skills and increase their vocabulary (Schienkman 2004). Oral class stories are perfect vehicles for practicing retelling.

Sherra's students, having already chosen symbols to represent each sentence in "Poppy's Visit" and told the story many times, are very familiar with the story. Sherra has a blank symbol grid displayed on an easel at the front of the room. She cuts the symbols on the original chart apart, places them on the empty grid in random order, and begins to tell the story out of sequence. Students immediately protest: "Mrs. Jones, you're telling the story the wrong way. That's not the way it goes!" Sherra says:

Class, you are so smart! You realized instantly that something was wrong. I was telling the details of the story, but not in the order that they happened. That's why the story did not make sense. Watch how I move the symbols around so that they are in the correct order. Now watch me check myself by retelling the story to see if it makes sense.

The students, in pairs, then cut up their own copies of the "Poppy's Visit" symbol chart, mix the symbols up, reorder them sequentially, and practice retelling the story to each other (see Figure 5.1).

Sherra then helps her students understand that the events in a familiar storybook have to be retold in the correct order for the story to make sense:

Figure 5.1 "Poppy's Visit" Sequenced Symbol Grid

> Just like you used symbols to help you retell "Poppy's Visit," you can use pictures to help you remember how a particular book goes. Watch me do that with one of our favorite stories, Old Bear, by Jane Hissey.

Sherra retells the first three pages of the book using the pictures to jog her memory. On the fourth page, she asks students to turn and tell a partner what happens next. Then she continues retelling the story using only the pictures and her own words, making sure students realize she is not reading the words in the book but is using the illustrations to help her remember how the story goes. When she finishes, she sends the students off to read a story independently and retell it to their reading partner using the illustrations.

Next, Sherra types up "Poppy's Visit," makes a copy for each pair of students, cuts the sentences apart, mixes them up, and distributes them to the student partners in a plastic baggie. Each partnership rebuilds the story in the correct order and reads it together as a shared reading. The next day, students try this work independently, sequencing the sentence strips and reading the story silently. Even though there are difficult words in the story, they are able to read with accuracy and at an appropriate rate because they know the story by heart. They are also able to read with expression, paying attention to punctuation.

Finally, Sherra has students glue the sentence strips in the correct order on a sheet of construction paper (see Figure 5.2) and sends them out to share the story in the wider world. Some students visit kindergarten classrooms, some seek out the principal, others find an audience in the media center. Then they all take the story home to read to their parents.

Students move from sequencing symbols to sequencing text.

Developing Vocabulary

A rich vocabulary is essential if children are to understand what they hear and read in school. It's also the key to communicating successfully with others. Research studies show a strong link between a well-developed vocabulary and school success. Therefore, in building a class story, we stock it with a few vocabulary words we want our students to learn.

The three vocabulary words Sherra introduces in "Poppy's Visit" are *reluctant*, *coaxed*, and *trellis*. Because the students have participated in the experience on which

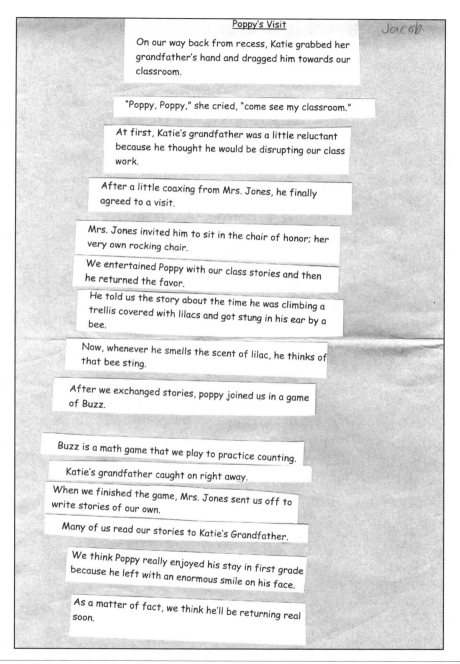

Poppy's Visit

Jacob

On our way back from recess, Katie grabbed her grandfather's hand and dragged him towards our classroom.

"Poppy, Poppy," she cried, "come see my classroom."

At first, Katie's grandfather was a little reluctant because he thought he would be disrupting our class work.

After a little coaxing from Mrs. Jones, he finally agreed to a visit.

Mrs. Jones invited him to sit in the chair of honor; her very own rocking chair.

We entertained Poppy with our class stories and then he returned the favor.

He told us the story about the time he was climbing a trellis covered with lilacs and got stung in his ear by a bee.

Now, whenever he smells the scent of lilac, he thinks of that bee sting.

After we exchanged stories, poppy joined us in a game of Buzz.

Buzz is a math game that we play to practice counting.

Katie's grandfather caught on right away.

When we finished the game, Mrs. Jones sent us off to write stories of our own.

Many of us read our stories to Katie's Grandfather.

We think Poppy really enjoyed his stay in first grade because he left with an enormous smile on his face.

As a matter of fact, we think he'll be returning real soon.

Figure 5.2 "Poppy's Visit" Sequenced Sentence Strips

the story is based, they implicitly understand what the words mean. When Katie dragged her grandfather to the classroom, he shook his head "no" and waved his hands back and forth—that's what *reluctant* looks like. When Sherra coaxed Poppy into the classroom, she motioned him to enter and told him it would be just fine— that's what being *coaxed* looks like. When Poppy told the story about climbing the lilac-covered trellis and being stung by a bee, the children asked what a trellis looked like. He made a climbing gesture with his hands as he explained. They used that gesture to represent the sentence in the story.

To make these words stick, Sherra lists them on chart paper and encourages students to use them in their conversation and their writing and notice them in books (see Figures 5.3 and 5.4). Each time a student uses or finds one of the words, he or she puts a tally mark next to it. Sherra also reads aloud books that include these words.

Figure 5.3 Jacob illustrates the word *coaxed*.

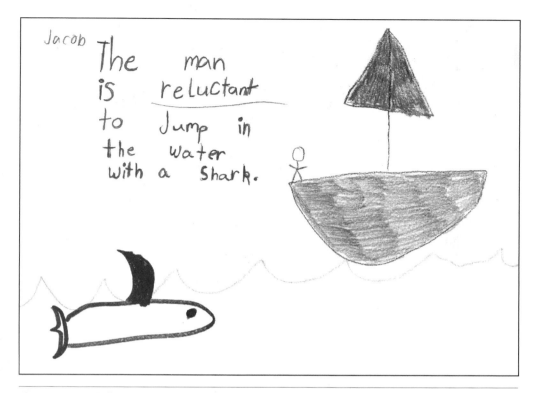

Figure 5.4 Jacob illustrates the word *reluctant*.

Paying Attention to Punctuation

Punctuation provides clues to the structure and organization of written language as well as the appropriate intonation and rhythm to use when reading aloud. Not observing punctuation reduces comprehension. Beginning and early readers tend to read right through punctuation. The class story is a perfect place to model that paying attention to punctuation is what smart readers do.

For example, Sherra displays the symbol page for "Poppy's Visit" and tells the story as if there are no periods. When students giggle, Sherra explains that it sounds funny because she never stopped after reading each sentence: "Every symbol represents one sentence. I am going to tell the story again and I am going to touch each symbol as I say that sentence. After I say each sentence, I am going to stop for just a moment before moving on to the next sentence. Ready, here I go."

She then tells the story one more time, this time asking students to identify where the periods should go: "Every time you think I have come to the end of a sentence and I should stop, stomp your foot on the ground and shout "period!"

Next Sherra passes out to each student a printed copy of the class story in which no periods are included. "I purposefully left out the periods in the class story. I want us to read the story together. We won't stop anywhere because there are no periods to tell us to stop." The class participates in a choral reading and laughs at how silly it sounds.

Using a document camera, Sherra rereads the story and inserts periods where they need to go. Then she has them do this on their individual copies. Almost every student is able to do this successfully (see the example in Figure 5.5). They are working with a class story they know by heart and have already practiced the task "in the air."

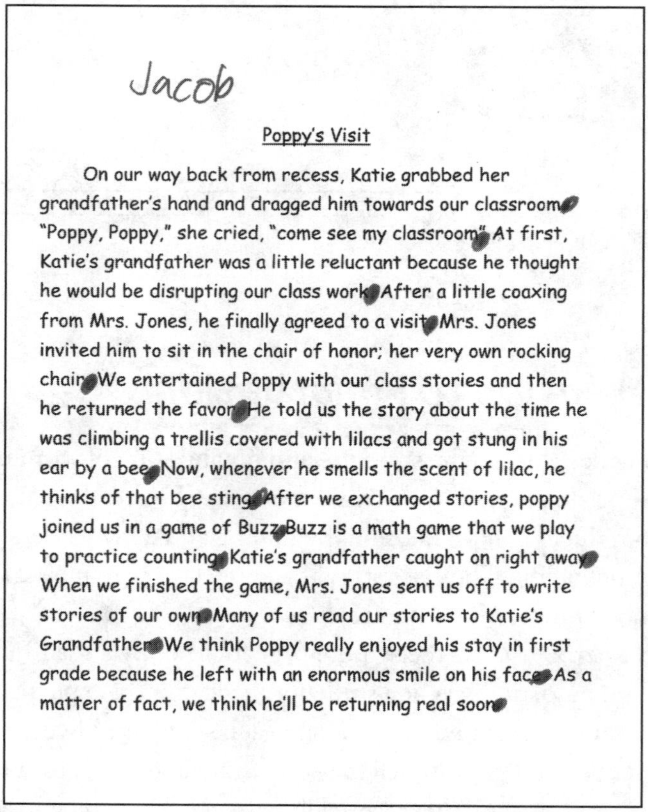

Jacob

Poppy's Visit

On our way back from recess, Katie grabbed her grandfather's hand and dragged him towards our classroom. "Poppy, Poppy," she cried, "come see my classroom." At first, Katie's grandfather was a little reluctant because he thought he would be disrupting our class work. After a little coaxing from Mrs. Jones, he finally agreed to a visit. Mrs. Jones invited him to sit in the chair of honor; her very own rocking chair. We entertained Poppy with our class stories and then he returned the favor. He told us the story about the time he was climbing a trellis covered with lilacs and got stung in his ear by a bee. Now, whenever he smells the scent of lilac, he thinks of that bee sting. After we exchanged stories, poppy joined us in a game of Buzz. Buzz is a math game that we play to practice counting. Katie's grandfather caught on right away. When we finished the game, Mrs. Jones sent us off to write stories of our own. Many of us read our stories to Katie's Grandfather. We think Poppy really enjoyed his stay in first grade because he left with an enormous smile on his face. As a matter of fact, we think he'll be returning real soon.

Figure 5.5 Punctuated Class Story

To prompt students to pay attention to periods in their independent reading, Sherra says, "Boys and girls, just like we had to stop at periods while reading the class story, we have to stop at periods while reading our books. In order to stop at a period, you have to notice that the period is there. So every day as you read your books, be on the lookout for periods. When you see one—*stop*!"

(This same procedure can be used to demonstrate how smart readers react to question marks, exclamation marks, and quotation marks.)

Finding and Using Text-Based Evidence

Students need to learn how to revisit text to support their thinking, especially when taking standardized tests. We help students develop this skill by presenting them with questions that can only be answered by having read the text. This can easily be done using a class story because the meaning has already been negotiated. We compile some explicit and implicit text-dependent questions and have students answer those questions using only the symbols from the story.

For example, Sherra asks, "In 'Poppy's Visit,' what word describes how Poppy felt before entering the classroom?" Most students know the answer without referring to the text, but Sherra insists that the student answering point to the symbol that represents the sentence in which the word appears.

Then she asks an implicit question: "Why did I call my rocking chair 'the chair of honor'?" The answer has to be inferred, but it can still be supported with evidence. Sherra guides her students to point to the symbol that represents the sentence *Mrs. Jones invited Poppy to sit in the chair of honor, her very own rocking chair.* She explains, "The rocking chair is my chair and I am the teacher in this classroom. I am usually the only person to sit in that chair, so I referred to it as a 'chair of honor.' " (Figure 5.6 lists some additional comprehension questions about "Poppy's Visit.") Next, Sherra now shows her students the story in print. Using the same comprehension questions, she guides them to highlight the words, phrases, or sentences that provide evidence for their answers.

It's not as easy for our students to answer comprehension questions about stories they don't know as well as class stories, but most understand what they are being asked to do. We begin by asking questions they can answer based on evidence in the illustrations, then move on to evidence in the printed text. We continually remind students that this is the same kind of detective work they did in their class stories.

Jacob

Comprehension Questions for "Poppy's Visit"

1. According to the story, what word describes how poppy felt when Katie first asked him to come in the classroom? reluctant

2. Who is the main character? poppy

3. What reminds poppy of the time he was stung by a bee? the smell of lilacx

4. In your opinion, why does Mrs. Jones refer to the rocking chair as "the chair of honor?" the rocking Chair is where mrs. Jones sits when she is teaching.

5. What do poppy and Mrs. Jones' class have in common? Storytelling

Figure 5.6 Comprehension Questions Based on "Poppy's Visit"

Visualizing

Visualizing is creating a vivid picture in one's mind based on what one reads—using sights, sounds, smells, tastes, and feelings to create a mental image that will help in remembering key details from the story. So that students understand this process, we think through the process aloud. For example, telling "Poppy's Visit," Sherra reads part of the story and then explains to students how she "makes a movie in her head":

[Reading the story] On our way back from recess, Katie grabbed her grandfather's hand and dragged him toward our classroom. "Poppy, Poppy," she cried, "come see my classroom." At first, Katie's grandfather was a little reluctant because he thought he would be disrupting our class work. After a little coaxing from Mrs. Jones, he finally agreed to a visit. *[End reading part of the story]*

> Boys and girls, I am going to stop here to make a movie in my head about what has happened so far. Here's how I do it: Our whole class was walking back to the classroom from recess. I can see us all walking in a line. Katie's grandfather was walking with us. All of a sudden, I saw Katie grab her grandfather's hand and yell in a loud voice, "Poppy, Poppy, come see my classroom." I noticed that Poppy was shaking his head no. I heard him explaining to Katie that he didn't want to disrupt our class work. That's when I decided to step in. I used my pointer finger to beckon him over to me. Then I coaxed him into the classroom by assuring him he was welcome.
>
> Now let's continue the story.

She does so, stopping from time to time to model visualization. When she finishes, she explains that this new "trick" will help them remember all the important parts of a story. Then she tells the story again, stopping at the same places, this time inviting her students to turn and visualize with a partner.

When we prompt students to use visualization in their independent reading, we continually stress that they have done this before in connection with class stories, and we encourage them to draw pictures of one element of the story at a time (setting, problem, solution).

Identifying the Beginning, Middle, and End

There are three essential parts to a story. The beginning defines the setting and sets the mood; a good beginning makes the reader want to read more. The middle includes the details of what takes place. The end is where the story comes to a close—there is a resolution.

Identifying the beginning, middle, and end of a story can be tricky for younger students, and using the class story makes the task less daunting. For example, Sherra first lists the three big happenings in "Poppy's Visit" on chart paper:

1. Poppy left happy.
2. We shared some stories, we played a math game, and we wrote some stories to share with Poppy.
3. After recess, Poppy reluctantly came into our classroom and sat in the rocking chair.

She then reads these sentences aloud and asks her students to turn and talk with a partner about which represents the beginning of the story, the middle of the story, and the end of the story. When they finish, she shares their smart thinking.

Next, she displays the symbol page that she and the students prepared for the story: "Boys and girls, I am going to tell this story pointing to each symbol as I go. When you think I have finished telling the beginning of the story, tell me to stop. Remember, the beginning only tells about Poppy reluctantly entering our classroom and sitting down in the rocking chair." The students tell her to stop after the fifth symbol, when Poppy takes a seat in the rocking chair. Sherra covers the first five symbols with blue sticky notes and identifies this section as the beginning of the story.

Then she identifies the middle and end of the story in the same way, covering the eight middle symbols with pink sticky notes and the two symbols representing the end with yellow sticky notes. The students now have a color-coded visual of the beginning, middle, and end of the class story.

During the week they do the following:

1. Students participate in a class discussion of how much longer the middle of a story is compared with the beginning or the end (which is easy to see because of the color-coded visual).

2. They line up to tell the story. Five students are needed to tell the beginning, eight to tell the middle, and two to tell the ending. After the students tell the story all the way through, Sherra plays around with the concept of beginning, middle, and ending by manipulating the participants. For example, she may tell students, "If you took part in telling the middle of the story, please sit down. Let's try telling the story again with only the people that are standing [the beginning and ending]." Another option would be to ask the beginning and ending to sit down while the students left standing tell only the middle.

3. Students create a three-box graphic organizer. In the first box, they illustrate the beginning of the story (Poppy coming). In the third box, they illustrate the end of the story (Poppy going). Then Sherra leads a discussion about what should go in the middle box: "Boys and girls, a lot of things happened in the middle and I am not sure how to fit all of that information in the middle box. Let me think. We shared stories with Poppy, we played a math game, and we wrote stories to read to Poppy. That's three happenings. I think I will divide the middle box into three parts and draw a picture for each happening in each smaller section." She models doing so, and the students follow suit on their own paper.

4. Using the three-box graphic organizer, they write the beginning, middle, and end of the story. (Sherra conducts a guided practice for a small group that isn't ready to do this on their own.)

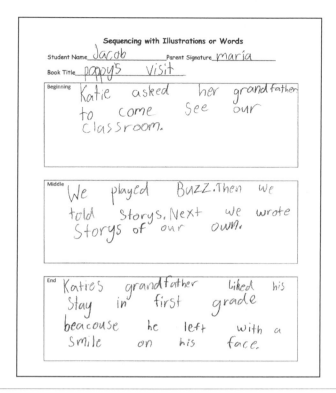

Figure 5.7 Jacob's Beginning, Middle, and End Graphic Organizer

Once our students get a feel for determining the beginning, middle, and end of several class stories, we monitor small groups of students as they apply this strategy to other books. The group reads a story; identifies the beginning, middle, and end; and determines the key elements to include in each box of a three-box organizer. (See the example in Figure 5.7.)

Finally, we turn the work over to students individually. We read a story aloud and ask students to record (in words or with drawings) the beginning, middle, and end of the story in the three boxes of a graphic organizer.

Summarizing

Summarization strategies are used in almost every content area. To summarize, students must determine the most important ideas in a text, omitting irrelevant information, and then tell or write those ideas in the sequence they occurred. Teaching students to summarize improves their memory of what they read.

For example, Sherra begins her instruction on summarizing by reading a summary on the back or inside cover of a book and defining what a summary is:

> Boys and girls, when you summarize a story, you are telling what the story is mostly about. It is different from a retelling where many of the key details are included. Let me read the summary of this book again. Do you see how the author just told what the book is mostly about and left out all of the juicy details? Now let's look at our class story. I am going to use sticky notes to cover all the juicy details on our symbol chart.

She then works her way through the story, thinking aloud as she decides which symbols to cover (those representing dialogue, elaboration, and similes, for example). When she finishes, only the symbols that tell the gist of the story—five out of fifteen—remain uncovered. She recites the sentences the uncovered symbols represent, which are the essence of the story. Finally, she demonstrates putting that information into her own words to create a summary: "One day, Katie's grandfather came to visit our class. We shared stories, played a game, and did some writing. He seemed happy when he left." Students then attempt to write their own summary of the class story (see Figure 5.8).

After practicing summarizing, students apply this newly learned technique to their own reading. They read a few pages in their book and mark the place to stop with a sticky note. Then they return to where they started and summarize what they just read. This exercise in determining importance lets them practice expressing key details and finding the main ideas. This same procedure is then applied to students' independent reading; we monitor a student's ability to summarize during individual reading conferences.

Identifying Story Elements

Understanding the way reading material is organized is important to comprehension. According to Dickson et al. (1998), teaching the elements of narrative (characters, setting, problems, solutions to the problems, and so on) gives students a frame of reference for processing and storing information. Irvin (1998) identifies awareness of text structures as an important metacognitive skill.

It is relatively simple to explain setting, characters, problem, and solution, especially in connection with a class story, because every student has experienced

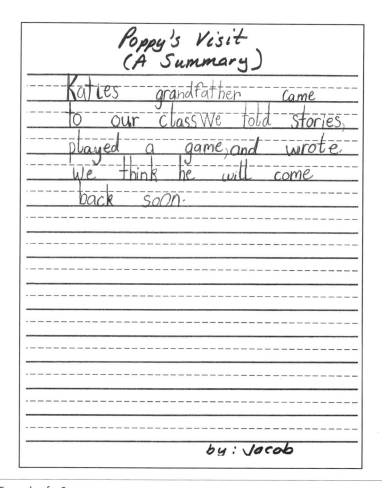

Figure 5.8 Example of a Summary

firsthand the occurrence that the story recounts. When Sherra asks her students where "Poppy's Visit" takes place (or asks them to identify any other story element), all eighteen hands in the classroom fly into the air. The students don't need to recall a story they either listened to or read; they only need to think back on a direct experience.

After identifying the story elements in a class story we have students:

» Record the setting, characters, problem, and/or solution using illustrations
» Record the setting, characters, problem, and/or solution using print

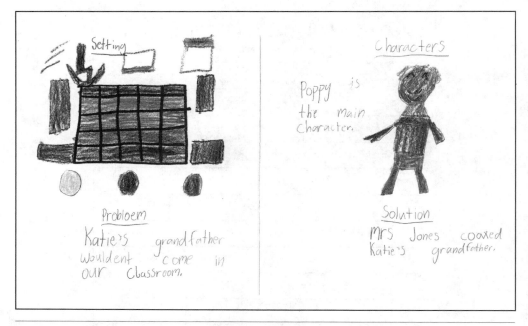

Figure 5.9 Story Elements

» Discuss the setting, characters, problem and/or solution with a partner, providing practice with speaking and listening skills

Once students have a firm understanding of story elements, it's easier for them to identify them in the books they read individually (see Figure 5.9).

Identifying Character Traits

Lessons on how to identify character traits introduce students to the comprehension strategy of making inferences. Rarely do authors explicitly state what a character is like inside. Readers must figure out these traits by studying the character's actions and interactions and the things she or he says. Using a class story, we teach our students to:

» Describe internal ("inside") and external ("outside") character traits
» Understand that characters grow and change
» Compare and contrast characters within a text or a series

Describing Internal and External Character Traits

Sherra sets out to teach her students to describe Poppy's "inside" and "outside" traits using evidence from the story. First, she asks her students to turn and talk about what Poppy looks like. The room buzzes with descriptions: old, short, gray hair, silver glasses, tattoo, and so on. Sherra lists these traits on chart paper. Next, she places a copy of the story on the document camera and challenges her students to find evidence for these descriptions. They quickly realize that their descriptions come from their having met Poppy in person, not from the story.

Next, they turn and talk about Poppy's inside character traits. Again, the room is abuzz: nice, kind, funny, a lover of stories, a good grandfather, a good listener, smart. Again, Sherra lists their descriptions and challenges them to find evidence in the text to support their answers. Students eagerly share their thoughts: "I know Poppy is a lover of stories because he listened to our stories and then he told us one of his own." "I know Poppy is smart because he caught on to how to play our math game right away." "I know Poppy's a good grandfather because he came to visit Katie at school and he was holding her hand." Students find this task amazingly simple when they own every piece of a story.

Understanding That Characters Grow and Change

In another lesson, Sherra highlights the beginning and the end of "Poppy's Visit" on the symbol chart. Then she leads a discussion.

> Boys and girls, do you remember how Poppy felt at the beginning of the story? He was sort of shy and reluctant to come into the classroom. Remember he was afraid that he would disrupt our class work? But look way down here at the end of the story. By the time Poppy left, he had an enormous smile on his face. Remember we all felt he would come back real soon? Now I want you to spend a few minutes studying the middle of the story. Think about what happened in the middle of this story to change the way that Poppy felt. Then, in your response journal, please make a list of reasons you think that Poppy changed from shy and reluctant at the beginning to extremely happy at the end.

Students attack their journals. They know the reasons Poppy changed and are eager to show off their knowledge: "Mrs. Jones coaxed Poppy into the room." "Mrs. Jones gave Poppy her rocking chair." "Poppy liked listening to our stories." "Poppy liked telling us a story." "Poppy liked playing our math game."

Comparing and Contrasting Characters

In yet another lesson, Sherra and her students compare and contrast the main character, Poppy, with a secondary character, Katie, using a Venn diagram. A student example is shown in Figure 5.10.

To prompt students to transfer this strategy to their independent reading, Sherra does the following:

» She leads discussions of character traits in which students support their opinions by dipping back into a story to study a character's actions and interactions and what she or he says.

» She leads discussions about how a character changes or grows throughout a story. Again, students refer to the book they are reading as they determine a character's motivation to change based on evidence in the story.

» She helps them use a Venn diagram or some other graphic organizer to compare and contrast characters.

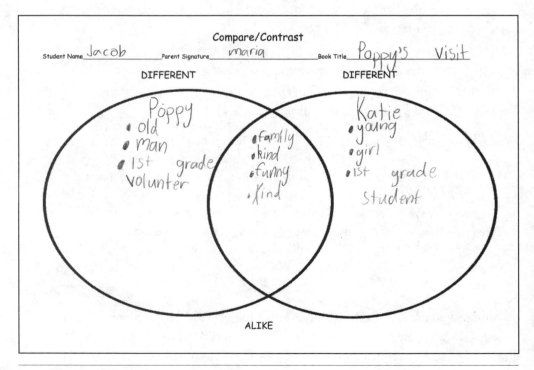

Figure 5.10 Compare and Contrast

Inferring

Inferring is typically defined as reading between the lines. The strategy usually involves:

» Forming a best guess using context clues, picture clues, and so forth
» Making predictions
» Drawing conclusions
» Finding the meaning of unknown words

Because Sherra's first graders have a solid understanding of what she means by text-based evidence, it's easy for her to present a definition and process for inferring:

> Boys and girls, remember the other day when you were describing Poppy's inside character traits and looking for evidence to support your thinking? Well, many of you said that Poppy was a good grandfather. Oddly enough, those words never appear in the story. What you did was, you looked at some evidence in the story and made your best guess. In your mind you were probably thinking, "Well, Poppy did come to visit Katie at school, he was holding her hand on the way back from recess, and he agreed to come into the classroom even though he was reluctant. I am going to guess that he is a good grandfather."

As Sherra presents other examples of reading between the lines, students start to catch on. She just needs to label the strategy and practice inferring using several more class stories before using the strategy with written texts.

Students need many opportunities to practice the skill of inferring, in small groups and independently. In our one-to-one conferences, we always use a class story as an anchor text and remind students often of the inferences they have made based on it.

Oral Class Stories in Whole-Class Reading Lessons

Just as with writing minilessons, we found that when planning reading minilessons around class stories, most of them fell into these categories:

» Foundational: Lessons support foundational ideas about reading and being a reader.
» Operational: Lessons support elements of the reading process.

» Print awareness: Lessons support print awareness, decoding, conventions, and grammar.

» Craft: Lessons support readers as they notice craft moves in their texts. (Dierking and Jones 2003)

Our minilesson work stands on the shoulders of the work done by Lucy Calkins and her colleagues at The Reading and Writing Project.

Next, you'll see a minilesson from each category, followed by a selection of sample teaching points for each lesson using the class story as a mentor. You can also use teaching points from these minilessons when conferring with individual readers or working with small groups.

1. Reading—Foundational

Minilesson: Reading with Determination

MATERIALS: FORMER ORAL CLASS STORY, LEVELED READERS FOR EACH PARTNERSHIP

Connect

Remind students that retelling class stories was difficult in the beginning, and that they needed to be determined and keep trying. Tell the class story together, and then tell students that just as they were determined to learn that class story, readers can use determination when they are reading because this helps them practice strategies that make them stronger readers.

Teach

Tell a story about someone reading with determination.

Model how to read with determination, sounding out words, looking at the pictures, and so forth. Tell students that when they read with determination, they can: (1) Look carefully at the pictures to help you, (2) use what you know about words, and (3) don't give up.

Active Engagement

Ask students to read books you've chosen for them in partnerships, using determination and working together to tackle tricky parts.

Link

Remind students to use everything you know about words and books and give reading a go, even if the book is new or feels tricky. Just as they learned the class story, they can be determined and learn to read their books.

2. Reading—Operational

Minilesson: Defining Story Elements

MATERIALS: ORAL CLASS STORY, SHORT NARRATIVE TEXT

Connect

Tell a story about noticing story elements when reading a familiar story aloud (a familiar fairy tale works well).

Teach

Choral tell any former oral class story.

Use the oral class story to define the setting, character, events leading to a problem or happening, and solution or ending to the story. As you define the elements, count them across your fingers.

Active Engagement

Choose a very short, predictable story to read to the class, and ask students to listen for the setting, character, events that lead to a big happening or problem, and solution or end to the story.

Ask students to turn and talk about the story elements. Listen in to coach students who are having trouble remembering the parts. Call students back together and share the elements of the book you read aloud.

Link

Tell students that paying attention to story elements helps readers when they tell a story and when they read a story. Story elements help readers hold onto the meaning and understand the story. Encourage students to stop after they have read a just-right book, or even one chapter of a chapter book, to note the story elements.

3. Reading—Print Awareness

Minilesson: Using Words We Know to Decode New Words

MATERIALS: SIMPLE DIAGRAM OF STAR CONSTELLATIONS THAT INCLUDES THE BIG AND LITTLE DIPPER, WHITE BOARDS AND MARKERS FOR EACH PARTNERSHIP, CHART PAPER, PREVIOUS CLASS STORY

Connect

Tell a story about noticing stars in the sky, and show students a constellation diagram. Point out a few constellations. Tell students that you can use one constellation to help you identify another.

Point out the Big Dipper, and show students how the last star of the handle is the first star of the Little Dipper.

Tell students that this same idea works with words, that readers use what they know about some words to help them read new words.

Teach

Display a sentence from a familiar class story written on a chart. You'll have underlined two words.

Demonstrate using parts of the words you've underlined to decode another; for example, if the sentence is *Yesterday we rushed inside from the P.E. field because it started to rain*, you might have underlined *st* from the word *started* and *ain* from the word *rain*. If I use the /st/ from *started* and /ain/ from *rain*, I can build a new word, *stain*. Write this on chart paper and say, "By using what I knew about two familiar words we were able to learn a new word." You could use any sentence to model this as long as it is from a previous class story, not one you are currently telling.

Active Engagement

Show students another familiar sentence and, after reading it together, tell students that they can work in partnerships with white boards to use what they know about two words in that sentence to make another word.

Circulate as partnerships are writing, and make a list to share with students of the new words they are making. Share all the new words formed with the class.

Link

Remind students that readers can always use words they already know how to read to help with new words they aren't sure of.

4. Reading—Craft

Minilesson: Finding Patterns in the Stories That You Read

MATERIALS: FORMER ORAL CLASS STORY THAT CONTAINS A PATTERN, CHART PAPER, FAMILIAR PICTURE BOOK

Connection

Tell students about patterns you've noticed in the world, and teach them that finding patterns in books will help them read books more fluently and help figure out words they might not know.

Teach

Retell an oral class story containing a pattern. Ask students to notice the pattern.

Next, read aloud the book that you have chosen and stop after a few pages; then think aloud, asking, "Does this book have a pattern?" Once students have noticed the pattern, ask them to describe how it works and what they predict will come next, using the pattern. Read on to verify their prediction.

Active Engagement

Give each partnership a small book containing a pattern. Have them work together to find the pattern by stopping after each page and asking, "Does this book have a pattern?" and "What is the pattern?"

Circulate as students are reading and record the different types of patterns noted in their small books. Once students have completed their books together, share the different types of patterns found. Then reiterate why finding a pattern can be helpful in reading and understanding a book.

Link

Remind students that every day when they are reading their own books they can ask themselves the two questions about patterns: "Does this book have a pattern? What is the pattern?" Also remind them that they included a pattern to help their listener enjoy and better understand their oral story. Authors of books do the same thing.

Sample Reading Teaching Points Using Class Stories as Mentors

FOUNDATIONAL

- Using the symbol grid from a familiar class story to demonstrate, show students how touching the pictures and saying how the story goes can help readers retell a book.
- Using the class story as a model, teach students that readers read their stories at a just-right rate so they are able to understand and remember the story or information in their books.
- Using the class story to demonstrate, teach students that readers read books with a storytelling voice by reading with enthusiasm and expression.
- Using the class story and symbol grid to practice, teach students that readers hold onto their stories by going back and retelling parts of the story to themselves.
- Using the class story to demonstrate, teach students that readers can choose a favorite page in a book they are reading to share with a partner as a way to learn more about books they might want to read themselves.
- Using a class story to model, teach students that readers can use their own stories to help understand someone else's stories by thinking about how their own story is alike or different from the book they are reading.

PRINT AWARENESS

- Using part of a familiar class story to demonstrate, teach students that readers blend sounds together to make a word by saying the sounds out loud slowly, and then saying them faster to blend them together.
- Using a sentence from a familiar class story, teach students that readers read across a word by looking closely at every single letter.
- Using a class story as a model, teach students that readers notice when the words they are reading don't make sense.

CRAFT

- Using a familiar class story to demonstrate, teach students that readers infer to make sense of what they are reading.
- Using a class story as a model, teach students that authors make readers wonder on purpose, because asking questions is an important skill that readers use to understand what they are reading.

Using Class Stories in Literacy Centers

Our students love to "muck about" telling and writing class stories in the literacy center. (We don't use a class story in the literacy center until it has been practiced, polished, performed, and celebrated—until students know the story so well we are able to use it as mentor text.) We introduce center activities one at a time and then allow a few weeks of guided practice, after which we add it to the center menu. As the menu grows, students' choices grow, but the menu is fluid and always subject to change. Here is a list of fifteen potential literacy center activities:

1. Write a class story individually or with a partner.
2. Elaborate on parts of a story that we didn't provide details about when we created the story.
3. Record a class story and relive it as a readers' theatre.
4. Make a book of the story.
5. Illustrate the setting of a story.
6. Draw the main character in a story and list some of his or her traits.
7. Mix up story sentence strips and put them back in order.
8. Write a letter to one of the characters in a story.
9. Use favorite vocabulary from a story to write and/or illustrate new sentences.
10. Create a different symbol page for a class story.
11. Make puppets to perform a class story.
12. Write a sequel to a class story.
13. Make a flipbook of the beginning, middle, and end of the story.
14. Create a page of your own "Mad Libs" that allow for substitutions of nouns and verbs based on a class story.
15. Create a kit for retelling a class story using pictures from a magazine or the Internet.

Joshua created a wordless book during center time using the class story, "Wiggle, Wiggle, Wiggle" (see Figure 5.11).

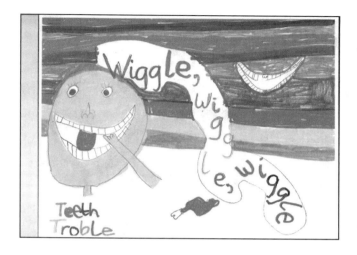

Wiggle, Wiggle, Wiggle! All morning long Joshua's tooth wouldn't come out. Wiggle, Wiggle, Wiggle! All through lunch Joshua's tooth wouldn't come out. Wiggle, Wiggle, Wiggle! All through music Joshua's tooth wouldn't come out. But after music . . . something exciting happened. First, Mrs. Jones said, "Joshua, your tooth is hanging on by a thread." Then the whole class started to chant, 'PULL IT, PULL IT, PULL IT.'" Joshua reached into his mouth and yanked the tooth out! He was so excited that Mrs. Jones let him call his mom on the phone. We all wondered what Joshua would get from the Tooth Fairy.

Figure 5.11 "Wiggle, Wiggle, Wiggle": A Class Story Illustrated by Joshua   *(continues)*

Figure 5.11 *(Continued)*

CHAPTER

Partnership and Individual Oral Stories

This chapter suggests four minilessons that help students find and tell a story, first with a partner and then on their own. They are just that: *suggestions*, not templates. The most successful minilessons are those you create for your own students and deliver in your own style. Pick and choose from these ideas as you design lessons that best serve your students. The goal is for students to find and tell the stories of their lives independently, using the same process they've followed as a class.

This approach to storytelling differs from writing personal narratives in writing workshop. Here students first tell the story orally. They build their stories using gestures and symbols to help them retrieve the same words each time. They may use rubrics as reminders to practice certain strategies. Once the story is built, they practice the story until they can tell it fluently. Only then do they put the story into print.

When emergent readers and writers try to record a story on paper, they have to attend to left-to-right orientation, spaces between words, letter/sound correspondence, punctuation, and sequencing, among many other things. Allowing students to be the teller of the tale before becoming the writer of the story scaffolds the writing process. Once student are confident "how the story goes," focusing on print awareness and conventions is much easier. Reluctant writers are eager to write a story they already know by heart, which paves the way for them to create and write stories independently.

When to move from class stories to partnership and individual stories depends on your students' prior storytelling experience, their language abilities, and how comfortable you are with the class story approach. We each spent several years implementing class stories before we felt ready to release the work of storytelling to our students.

Our work with partnership and individual stories does not replace writing workshop. We present the four initial minilessons during writing workshop; after that, we tuck the work in throughout the day.

Oral Partnership Stories

The main difference between class and partnership oral stories is that we don't find and build the story—the partners do. Another difference is that while class stories always remain oral, the partnership has to see their story in print to be able to practice it the same way every time.

We pair our students homogeneously to create balanced partnerships in which each student feels confident making storytelling decisions. Once partnerships are formed, we present explicit minilessons that teach students how to work together to identify a common shared experience suitable to become a story and then build that story. We emphasize decision making and compromise. Together, with a rubric to guide them, the partners answer such questions as, "How should we start the story?" "How should the story end?" "Where can we include dialogue?" "What other craft should we include?"

After the partners agree on the topic of their oral story, they schedule a conference. We listen to the story and record it in writing, then read it back exactly as they told it to us. After that we compliment something, teach something, and prompt active engagement. For example:

Partnership Story: *The other day at recess, Michaela and I were playing tag. We were chasing each other around a tree. All of a sudden, Michaela tripped over her shoelaces and fell down. "Ouch, I hurt my knee," she screamed. I took her to the clinic for a Band-Aid. When we returned to recess, Mrs. Manley said to Michaela, "Now you know why it is important to keep your shoes tied!"*

Compliment: I noticed you used dialogue in your story twice. The dialogue made me feel like I was right there with you.

Instruction: Today I would like to teach you another trick to make a story more interesting to the listener. It is called elaboration. When you elaborate, you tell more about the sentence before. Listen as I say this sentence: *As I was riding my bike down the sidewalk, I fell off and landed on my knee.* If I wanted to elaborate, I would have to tell more about that sentence. Listen as I give that a try. *As I was riding my bike*

down the sidewalk, I fell off and landed on my knee. I was scared to look down because I
thought I might see blood.

Active Engagement: Now it is your turn to try elaboration. Go back into the story where Michaela said, "Ouch, I hurt my knee." Talk to your partner and decide how you could tell more about that sentence.

When revisions have been made, we type the story on the computer exactly as the partners have told it. We cut the sentences apart, mix them up, and have the partners use the graphic organizer in Figure 6.1 (or Appendix A) to reorder the strips so the

The Story Sentence by Sentence	The Symbol	Is There a Gesture?

Figure 6.1 Story Recording Sheet (see Appendix A for reproducible version)

story makes sense, then we add symbols and decide on gestures. Students glue the sentences, in order, in the first column; draw a symbol to represent each sentence in the second column; and place an X in the third column indicating that a gesture has been created.

After the partners complete the graphic organizer, they practice the story by echo telling, choral telling, taking turns telling, and getting good at one sentence. The goal is to be able to fold the graphic organizer so the print is not visible and tell the story relying only on the symbols and gestures. The story is performance ready when both partners can tell the story fluently, without using the graphic organizer.

Minilesson 1: Being a Good Storytelling Partner

MATERIALS: A PREPARED PARTNERSHIP LIST THAT MATCHES STUDENTS OF LIKE ABILITIES OR PROVIDES SUPPORT TO ENGLISH LANGUAGE LEARNERS SO THAT THE PROCESS IS BALANCED

Connect

Remind your students of the work they've done all year to find shared experiences and turn them into oral stories. Tell them that today they'll have a chance to do this work with a partner. "Two people will work together to find a shared experience, tell it like a story, practice the story, and finally perform it for an audience. But before we start, I want to talk with you about being a good storytelling partner."

Teach

Tell students that it is important for partners to treat each other kindly and to show each other they are happy to work together. Remind them how important it is for partners to share the work. "Strong partnerships work as a team to find a story, tell the story, practice the story, and perform the story for an audience. Strong partners are encouraging and offer compliments to each other." With a student volunteer, model shaking hands and saying, "I am so happy to be your partner and I know we will have fun working together. I am going to do all I can to make our story fantastic!"

Active Engagement

Tell students that as you announce the storytelling partnerships, each pair can choose a spot in the classroom and spend a few minutes talking and getting to know each other. After a few minutes of this, call everyone back to the gathering area.

Link

Tell students that you loved watching them treat their partners with kindness and respect, and that tomorrow (or whenever the next session is) they will begin finding a story together.

Minilesson 2: Finding a Story with a Partner

MATERIALS: THE RUBRIC IN FIGURE 6.2 (OR APPENDIX B), IF YOU WISH TO USE IT (PRESENT A MINILESSON ON USING A RUBRIC WITH A PARTNER BEFORE YOU GET TO THIS POINT IF YOUR CLASS NEEDS DIRECT SUPPORT.)

Connect

Remind students of the work they did earlier getting to know their storytelling partner. Tell them that today they will get started on the work of finding a story that the partnership will eventually share with others. "Today, I am going to teach you how to go about the business of finding a story *together*."

Teach

"In order to find a story together, you are going to have to *be* together. In other words, the same experience won't happen to both of you if you are not near each other. So for the next several days, you are going to spend as much time with your partner as you can." When students spend time with their partners is up to you. You'll need to point out examples of good opportunities for partners to spend time together. For instance, in Sherra's classroom students are free to talk, read, write, color, or work on the computer for the first fifteen minutes each morning. That's a great time for partners to be together. You might also suggest spending time together at lunch, on the playground, during recess, walking to P.E., or working in a center. You can also deliberately assign time for partners to be together. (For example, have student partners return books to the library. Who knows what may happen or what they may notice on the way!)

Tell your students that as they spend time together, they should be on the lookout for a story, one that's about something that happens to both of them at the same time. Once they find a story, they'll work to tell it in the order that it happened. This will require making some decisions together. Then demonstrate this work for the students. Best-case scenario, you'll role-play with another teacher, but if need be, choose a student and rehearse with him or her beforehand.

Sherra modeled walking to the library with her partner, Sam. They pretended to hear a noise in a tree and looked up in the branches. Sherra pointed and said, "Do you see the bird in that nest? She's singing to us. I never noticed her before." Then she turned to Sam and said, "Hey, we could tell a story about noticing the bird in the nest."

Next, Sherra and Sam retold the event in the order it happened, modeling making decisions together. Their story went like this:

> Yesterday, Sam and I were walking to the library. All of a sudden, we heard a loud noise coming from the big oak tree. Sam and I looked up at the same time. We spotted a beautiful red bird sitting in a nest. "Wow, I never noticed that bird before," cried Sam. "It's almost like she's singing to us," I whispered. On the way back from the library, Sam and I looked for our new friend. Boo-hoo, she was nowhere in sight.

Active Engagement

Explain to students that you are going to give some examples of "happenings" that might become stories. Ask them to signal "thumbs up" if they think the incident sounds like a partnership story or "thumbs down" if they think it doesn't. Suggestions:

- » The time we ran to art because it started thundering and lightning
- » The time a storm blew the shed down at my house
- » The time my mom got mad at me for breaking a lamp
- » The time we both went to the principal's office to read

Link

Remind students that for the next several days, partners should spend as much time together as possible and be on the lookout for partner stories. Tell them that when they find a story, they will need to decide together how to tell the story in the order that it happened. Let them know that each partnership will meet with you in a conference and (if you choose to use the rubric in Figure 6.2 or Appendix B) that they'll use a rubric to help them decide what to include in their story.

Don't worry if several of your partnerships recognize the same incident as a potential story. Your entire class will often experience the same event. For instance, if you take the class outside for a Popsicle treat, two or three partnerships may use that as their story. That's okay; this is a teachable moment. It's interesting for the class to compare the way the stories are composed. You can examine the different leads, endings, word choices, and craft decisions.

Partners: _____   _____

Find a Story	Length of Story	Dialogue	Craft
3 Came from a shared experience	**3** At least 7 sentences long	**3** Dialogue used more than once	**3** Evidence of more than one craft
2 Came from the experience of one partner	**2** At least 5–6 sentences long	**2** Dialogue used one time	**2** Evidence of one craft
1 Did not come from a real-life experience	**1** Less than 5 sentences long	**1** Dialogue not used	**1** No evidence of craft

Total points _____

Figure 6.2 Partnership Rubric for Finding and Building an Oral Story (see Appendix B for reproducible version)

Minilesson 3: Revising a Story with a Partner

MATERIALS: THE RUBRIC IN FIGURE 6.2 (OR APPENDIX B), IF YOU WANT YOUR STUDENTS TO USE IT

Connect

Remind students of the work they've been doing over the last few days to find and compose a story. Let them know that soon you'll confer with each partnership to talk about ways to make their stories even stronger, but that today you want to teach them how to revise a story on their own to make it even stronger.

Teach

Tell students that revision simply means making a change in their story to make it stronger. Remind them that as they reread their story with their partner, they can ask, "Does our story come from a common experience? What could we add to this story to make it even better?"

Tell a partner story as you think aloud about how you might revise it. Sherra uses this story as an example:

> "Would you girls like to go read your poem to the principal?" asked Mrs. Jones. We grabbed our poetry folders and headed to the office. Mrs. Duncan was waiting for us at her desk. We read her the poem of the week, "Flashlights in the Dark." After we read the poem, she smiled and gave us each a rainbow-colored pencil. I guess she thought we did a good job.

After she tells the story she thinks aloud: "Let's see, the story is about something that happened to both of us. It's the story about the time we both went to read to the principal. Now let's count the sentences. Only six sentences! That means we'll need to add at least one sentence. Let's jot that down so we don't forget. We better check for dialogue. Are there at least two places in the story that we made people talk? We made our teacher ask a question right at the beginning of the story. Hey, that's also evidence of craft—starting a story with a question. That's the only place we used dialogue though. So we need at least one more sentence, and we need to make someone talk. That seems easy. Let's think. We already made our teacher talk. We could make her talk again or we could make one of us say something. We could even make the principal say something. Let's reread this story to look for a place that we can add dialogue."

After you make changes to your story, retell the story aloud to the class. If you're using a rubric and expect your students to do so as well, model explicitly checking the story against the rubric.

Active Engagement

Using the same story, ask students to turn and talk to their partner about something else they could revise. Suggest adding details, using alliteration—whatever your class is working on. After listening in, share a few of their good ideas.

Link

Remind students that they'll now revise their own story with their partner. If they're using the rubric, remind them to keep it handy as they work.

Minilesson 4: Practicing a Story with a Partner

MATERIALS: STORY RECORDING SHEET IN FIGURE 6.3 (OR APPENDIX C); THE RUBRIC IN FIGURE 6.4 (APPENDIX D), IF YOU WANT YOUR STUDENTS TO USE IT

Connect

Remind students of the work they've been doing in partnerships to find, compose, and revise a story. Tell them that today you want to teach them that storytellers practice and practice retelling their story to get them ready to share it with an audience.

Teach

Show students your example story on a story recording sheet (Figure 6.3), and add symbols and gestures to each line of the story. (Your students will be very familiar with this process, since they've done it so many times before with class stories.) Don't ask students for suggestions. Then say, "Did you see how quickly I did that? I added both symbols and gestures to each line of the story. Now I can use this sheet to help me practice the story." Give students their own story recording sheets and tell them that the symbols and gestures they choose will help them remember how the story goes.

Active Engagement

Ask students to talk with their partner about how they'll get started working on the recording sheet. What symbols and gestures might they use?

Link

Remind partners that they will both participate in adding symbols and gestures to their story using the recording sheet. If you are using the rubric in Figure 6.4, show students how to use it as they practice. Tell them that after a lot of practice, they will be able to stop reading the words and rely solely on the symbols and gestures to remember how the story goes. Demonstrate by folding back the words on your mentor story's recording sheet. Remind students to practice often using the symbols and gestures. Tell them their goal is to be able to tell the story the same way every time without using the recording sheet.

The Story Sentence by Sentence	The Symbol	Is There a Gesture?
"Would you girls like to read your poem to the principal?" asked Mrs. Jones.		
"We thought you would never ask!" we screamed at the same time.		
We grabbed our poetry folders and headed to the office.		
Mrs. Duncan was waiting at her desk.		
We read her the poem of the week, "Flashlights in the Dark."		
After we read the poem, she smiled and gave us each a rainbow-colored pencil.		
We guess she thought we did a good job.		

Figure 6.3 Story Recording Sheet Example (see Appendix C for reproducible version)

Partners: _____   _____

Symbols		Gestures		Telling the Story		Frequency	
3	Every sentence has a symbol	3	Every sentence has a gesture	3	Practiced using symbols *and* gestures	3	Practiced more than once a day
2	Some sentences have symbols	2	Some sentences have gestures	2	Practiced using symbols *or* gestures	2	Practiced once every day
1	Symbols were not created	1	Gestures were not created	1	Did not use symbols or gestures to practice	1	Did not practice every day

Total points _____

Figure 6.4 Partnership Rubric for Practicing an Oral Story (see Appendix D for reproducible version)

Individual Stories

After your students have built, practiced, and performed partnership stories, you may want to move on to individual oral stories (the gradual release instructional model). The main difference between partnership and individual stories is that students are not working collaboratively; the experience doesn't have to be shared and may have happened somewhere other than school. Maybe a student has a great story to share about something that happened at home, in the park, or on the beach. Even though each student is now responsible for all the work, the process is the same.

Each student will be on the lookout for an experience that can be turned into a story. Once they find a story, they will decide how they want their story to go. "How will it start? How will it end? Where and how often can I use dialogue? What other craft can I include?" After those decisions are made, the student will confer with you. As you listen to the story, you will jot it down on a piece of paper so you can tell it back to the student the same way she or he told it to you. You will find something to compliment and something to teach. You will coach the student to make revisions "in the air." Finally, you will type the story and cut the sentences apart. Using the graphic organizer in Figure 6.1 (or Appendix A), the student will sequence the sentences, create symbols, and decide on gestures. Finally, he or she will practice the story until it is performance ready.

Students may find the following three rubrics useful as they build, practice, and perform their individual oral stories.

Name: _____

Find a Story		Length of Story		Dialogue		Craft	
3	Came from a personal experience	3	At least 7 sentences long	3	Dialogue used more than once	3	Evidence of more than one craft
2	Came from the experience of another person	2	At least 5–6 sentences long	2	Dialogue used one time	2	Evidence of one craft
1	Did not come from a real-life experience	1	Less than 5 sentences long	1	Dialogue not used	1	No evidence of craft

Total points _____

Figure 6.5 Individual Rubric for Finding and Building an Oral Story (see Appendix E for reproducible version)

Name: _____

Symbols		Gestures		Telling the Story		Frequency	
3	Every page has a symbol	3	Every page has a gesture	3	Practiced using symbols *and* gestures	3	Practiced more than once a day
2	Some pages have symbols	2	Some pages have gestures	2	Practiced using symbols *or* gestures	2	Practiced once every day
1	Symbols were not created	1	Gestures were not created	1	Did not use symbols or gestures to practice	1	Did not practice every day

Total points _____

Figure 6.6 Individual Rubric for Practicing an Oral Story (see Appendix F for reproducible version)

Name: _____

Accuracy		Rate		Expression		Volume/Eye Contact	
3	I tell the story the same way every time.	3	I tell the story smoothly and at a "just-right" rate.	3	I used my voice to tell the whole story in an exciting way.	3	I looked right at the audience and I was easy to hear.
2	I need a little more practice to tell the story the same way every time.	2	I am still sort of hesitant, so I sound too slow.	2	I used my voice to tell parts of the story in an exciting way.	2	I need to work on either volume or eye contact.
1	I would need a lot more practice to tell the story the same way every time.	1	My audience can't understand me because I was speaking too fast.	1	My voice did not change throughout the story.	1	I need to work on both volume and eye contact.

Total points _____

Figure 6.7 Individual Rubric for Presenting an Oral Story (see Appendix G for reproducible version)

In Conclusion

Partnership and individual stories are worth the time and effort that you and your students put into them. Your class will brim with students eager to show off their storytelling skills and share their written pieces. We celebrate the work by inviting parents in for a storytelling celebration. The students introduce themselves and entertain their parents with their performances. Afterward, each student shows their parents the story in written form. Students are proud, parents are impressed, and we're thrilled!

Conclusion *Class Stories and Beyond*

Final Thoughts

At a dinner given by a mutual friend, we began talking about our favorite storytellers—Rev. Vicki, Uncle Harry, Dr. Martin Luther King, Oprah, Maya Angelou—as well as several of our students. That year our district wanted every teacher to engage in some type of inquiry: Research a burning question and develop ideas for changing one's instruction. Overhearing our conversation, a colleague decided on the spot to pursue oral storytelling as her inquiry. When she asked why we do this work, we had a lot to say:

» Students are natural storytellers.

» Oral storytelling is easy to implement.

» Students become experts at finding the stories of their lives.

» Incorporating gestures and symbols helps students retrieve words.

» Students learn to tell longer and more sophisticated stories.

» Students experience the excitement of revision.

» Students become experts at inserting craft moves into their stories.

» Students learn to retell stories with fluency.

» Oral storytelling prompts the same teaching points that reading and writing instruction does.

» Storytelling is a good way to introduce new vocabulary.

» Storytelling is an efficient way to study language structure.

» Storytelling is an interesting way for students to play with words.

» Through storytelling, children practice conventions "in the air."

» Storytelling encompasses all the conditions of learning: immersion, demonstration, engagement, expectation, responsibility, approximation, practice, and response.

» Parents love listening to their children tell class stories.

» We have oral mentor texts to use when teaching reading and writing.

An oral class story capturing a shared experience is a powerful mentor text. Teaching children to be fluent storytellers is a worthy endeavor. Learning the class story helps students to do these things:

» Tell a story at a "just right" rate

» Tell a story using expression and rhythm

» Tell a story accurately, in the correct sequence

» Make eye contact with an audience

» Use a clear, audible voice

» Perform in front of an audience

» Hear what a story sounds like

» Learn new vocabulary

» Learn temporal words and story language

» Learn craft techniques

These are valuable speaking and listening skills, but why stop there? When you create, teach, and practice a class story, you have an oral mentor text that everyone in your class owns. You can pull it out at will and use it as a mentor text in whole-group and small-group instruction and in individual conferences. Any writing strategy or craft technique used in the class story will begin to appear in your students' individual writing. Any reading comprehension strategy you need to teach can be taught through one of these familiar texts. Literacy centers that revolve around class stories become stations for practicing the skills and concepts you want your students to internalize. Class stories are valuable, free resources for integrating curriculum, aligning your teaching with the Common Core State Standards, and meeting the needs of your particular students.

Final Story

One day, after Sherra picked up her first graders from P.E., Andrew exclaimed, "Mrs. Jones, please let me tell the class the funniest story that happened during P.E." As the class settled into the gathering area, she invited him to the front of the room. He began the story. As he spoke, Sherra was, first of all, impressed that he had noticed a small happening to be worthy of a retelling. He was able to retell his experience with accuracy, expression, and specific word choice. His story was told in the order that it happened, so it made sense. This is no small feat for a first grader. It was most certainly a story that the audience found humorous and enjoyable.

> As soon as we got to P.E., Mrs. Woodka asked, "Caleigh, did you remember the nutrition bag?" Caleigh realized that she had forgotten it in the classroom. Mrs. Woodka asked me if I would walk back to the classroom with Caleigh to get the bag. When we walked into the classroom, Mrs. Jones wasn't there. It was weird to be in the room without her. We started to look for the nutrition bag when all of a sudden, the phone rang. A voice kept calling out, "Cecily, Cecily, Cecily." Me and Caleigh did not know what to do. Finally I yelled, "Nobody is here; we're just kids." Then we grabbed the nutrition bag and ran out of the room. We laughed all the way back to P.E.

Throughout the day, Andrew told the story several more times. He shared the story with Mrs. Dierking, with the principal, with the P.E. teachers—and with Mrs. Graska Cecily, the teacher in the room next door that the office had been trying to locate over the intercom. This story circulated throughout the school like a viral video. Andrew couldn't wait to write that story during independent writing time. This story begged to be written! Sherra's heart soared. The organic nature of where this story was born, and how it took on a life of its own was truly beautiful. This is why we engage in storytelling . . . this is why we value the stories of our lives . . . this is why we implore you to jump on board.

Appendix A

Story Recording Sheet Template

The Story Sentence by Sentence	The Symbol	Is There a Gesture?

Appendix B

Partnership Rubric for Finding and Building an Oral Story

Partners: _____   _____

Find a Story		Length of Story		Dialogue		Craft	
3	Came from a shared experience	**3**	At least 7 sentences long	**3**	Dialogue used more than once	**3**	Evidence of more than one craft
2	Came from the experience of one partner	**2**	At least 5–6 sentences long	**2**	Dialogue used one time	**2**	Evidence of one craft
1	Did not come from a real-life experience	**1**	Less than 5 sentences long	**1**	Dialogue not used	**1**	No evidence of craft

Total points _____

Appendix C

Story Recording Sheet Example

The Story Sentence by Sentence	The Symbol	Is There a Gesture?
"Would you girls like to read your poem to the principal?" asked Mrs. Jones.		
"We thought you would never ask!" we screamed at the same time.		
We grabbed our poetry folders and headed to the office.		
Mrs. Duncan was waiting at her desk.		
We read her the poem of the week, "Flashlights in the Dark."		
After we read the poem, she smiled and gave us each a rainbow-colored pencil.		
We guess she thought we did a good job.		

Appendix D

Partnership Rubric for Practicing an Oral Story

Partners: _____   _____

Symbols		Gestures		Telling the Story		Frequency	
3	Every sentence has a symbol	3	Every sentence has a gesture	3	Practiced using symbols *and* gestures	3	Practiced more than once a day
2	Some sentences have symbols	2	Some sentences have gestures	2	Practiced using symbols *or* gestures	2	Practiced once every day
1	Symbols were not created	1	Gestures were not created	1	Did not use symbols or gestures to practice	1	Did not practice every day

Total points _____

Appendix E

Individual Rubric for Finding and Building an Oral Story

Name: _____

Find a Story		Length of Story		Dialogue		Craft	
3	Came from a personal experience	3	At least 7 sentences long	3	Dialogue used more than once	3	Evidence of more than one craft
2	Came from the experience of another person	2	At least 5–6 sentences long	2	Dialogue used one time	2	Evidence of one craft
1	Did not come from a real-life experience	1	Less than 5 sentences long	1	Dialogue not used	1	No evidence of craft

Total points _____

Appendix F

Individual Rubric for Practicing an Oral Story

Name: _____

Symbols		Gestures		Telling the Story		Frequency	
3	Every page has a symbol	3	Every page has a gesture	3	Practiced using symbols *and* gestures	3	Practiced more than once a day
2	Some pages have symbols	2	Some pages have gestures	2	Practiced using symbols *or* gestures	2	Practiced once every day
1	Symbols were not created	1	Gestures were not created	1	Did not use symbols or gestures to practice	1	Did not practice every day

Total points _____

Appendix G

Individual Rubric for Presenting an Oral Story

Name: _____

Accuracy		Rate		Expression		Volume/Eye Contact	
3	I tell the story the same way every time.	3	I tell the story smoothly and at a "just-right" rate.	3	I used my voice to tell the whole story in an exciting way.	3	I looked right at the audience and I was easy to hear.
2	I need a little more practice to tell the story the same way every time.	2	I am still sort of hesitant, so I sound too slow.	2	I used my voice to tell parts of the story in an exciting way.	2	I need to work on either volume or eye contact.
1	I would need a lot more practice to tell the story the same way every time.	1	My audience can't understand me because I was speaking too fast.	1	My voice did not change throughout the story.	1	I need to work on both volume and eye contact.

Total points _____

References

Ashton-Warner, Sylvia. 1963. *Teacher*. New York: Simon & Schuster.

Benson, Vicki, and Carrice Cummins. 2000. *The Power of Retelling: Developmental Steps for Building Comprehension*. New York: McGraw-Hill.

Brandi-Muller, Justine. 2005. "Retelling Stories." Accessed April 7, 2014. www.ldonline .org/article/13282?theme=print.

Bruner, Jerome S. 1985. *Child's Talk: Learning to Use Language*. New York: W.W. Norton & Company.

Calkins, Lucy, with colleagues from the Reading and Writing Project. 2003. *Units of Study for Primary Writing: A Yearlong Curriculum*. Portsmouth, NH: Heinemann.

Cambourne, Brian. 1998. *The Whole Story: Natural Learning and the Acquisition of Literacy in the Classroom*. New York: Scholastic.

Dickson, S. V., D. C. Simmons, and E. J. Kame'enui. 1998. "Text Organization: Research Bases." In *What Reading Research Tells Us About Children with Diverse Learning Needs*, edited by D. C. Simmons and E. J. Kame'enui, 239–278. Mahwah, NJ: Erlbaum.

Dierking, Connie, and Sherra Jones. 2003. *Growing Up Writing*. Gainesville, FL: Maupin House.

Dorn, Linda, and Carla Soffos. 2005. *Teaching for Deep Comprehension*. Portland, ME: Stenhouse.

Fountas, Irene C. and Gay Su Pinnell. 2006. *Teaching for Comprehending and Fluency: Thinking, Talking, and Writing About Reading, K–8*. Portsmouth, NH: Heinemann.

Gillard, Marni. 1996. *Storyteller, Storyteacher: Discovering the Power of Storytelling for Teaching and Living*. Portland, ME: Stenhouse.

Hart, Betty, and Todd Risley. 1995. *Meaningful Differences in the Everyday Experience of Young American Children*. Baltimore, MD: Paul H. Brooks Publishing Co.

Heard, Georgia. 1991. *Awakening the Heart: Exploring Poetry in Elementary and Middle School*. Portsmouth, NH: Heinemann.

Irvin, J. L. 1998. *Reading and the Middle School Student: Strategies to Enhance Literacy*. Boston: Allyn and Bacon.

Lee, Dorris May Lee, and R. V. Allen. 1963. *Learning to Read Through Experience*. Upper Saddle River, NJ: Prentice Hall.

National Governors Association Center for Best Practices, Council of Chief State School Officers. 2010. *Common Core State Standards*. Washington, DC: National Governors Association Center for Best Practices, Council of Chief State School Officers.

Nessel, Denise D., and Carol N. Dixon. 2008. *Using the Language Experience Approach with English Language Learners: Strategies for Engaging Students and Developing Literacy*. Thousand Oaks, CA: Corwin Press.

Owocki, Gretchen. 2003. *Comprehension: Strategic Instruction for K–3 Children*. Portsmouth, NH: Heinemann.

Paley, Vivian Gussin. 1990. *The Boy Who Would Be a Helicopter*. Boston: Harvard University Press.

Schienkman, N. 2004. "Picturing a Story." *Teaching PreK–8* 34 (6): 58–59.

Schwartz, Shanna. 2008. *A Quick Guide to Making Your Teaching Stick, K–5*. Portsmouth, NH: Heinemann.

Sulzby, Elizabeth. 1991. "Assessment of Emergent Literacy." *The Reading Teacher* 44 (7): 498–500.

Children's Books Cited

Cronin, Doreen. 2011. *Click Clack Moo: Cows That Type*. New York: Little Simon.

Henkes, Kevin. 2004. *Kitten's First Full Moon*. New York: HarperCollins.

Hissey, Jane. 1989. *Old Bear*. New York: Random House.

Munsch, Robert. 1996. *Stephanie's Ponytail*. Toronto, Canada: Annick Press.

———. 2002. *Andrew's Loose Tooth*. New York: Scholastic.

Prelutsky, Jack. 1980. "Spaghetti, Spaghetti." In *Rainy Rainy Saturday*. New York: HarperCollins.

Wells, Rosemary. 1985. *Max's Birthday*. New York: Dial Books for Young Readers.

Zweibel, Alan. 2005. *Our Tree Named Steve*. New York: Puffin.